Florida
Algebra I
EOC

SUCCESS STRATEGIES

Florida EOC Test
Review for the Florida
End-of-Course Exams

TABLE OF CONTENTS

Introduction

Thank you for purchasing this resource! You have made the choice to prepare yourself for a test that could have a huge impact on your future, and this guide is designed to help you be fully ready for test day. Obviously, it's important to have a solid understanding of the test material, but you also need to be prepared for the unique environment and stressors of the test, so that you can perform to the best of your abilities.

For this purpose, the first section that appears in this guide is the **Success Strategies**. We've devoted countless hours to meticulously researching what works and what doesn't, and we've boiled down our findings to the five most impactful steps you can take to improve your performance on the test. We start at the beginning with study planning and move through the preparation process, all the way to the testing strategies that will help you get the most out of what you know when you're finally sitting in front of the test.

We recommend that you start preparing for your test as far in advance as possible. However, if you've bought this guide as a last-minute study resource and only have a few days before your test, we recommend that you skip over the first two Success Strategies since they address a long-term study plan.

If you struggle with **test anxiety**, we strongly encourage you to check out our recommendations for how you can overcome it. Test anxiety is a formidable foe, but it can be beaten, and we want to make sure you have the tools you need to defeat it.

Success Strategy #1 – Plan Big, Study Small

There's a lot riding on your performance. If you want to ace this test, you're going to need to keep your skills sharp and the material fresh in your mind. You need a plan that lets you review everything you need to know while still fitting in your schedule. We'll break this strategy down into three categories.

Information Organization

Start with the information you already have: the official test outline. From this, you can make a complete list of all the concepts you need to cover before the test. Organize these concepts into groups that can be studied together, and create a list of any related vocabulary you need to learn so you can brush up on any difficult terms. You'll want to keep this vocabulary list handy once you actually start studying since you may need to add to it along the way.

Time Management

Once you have your set of study concepts, decide how to spread them out over the time you have left before the test. Break your study plan into small, clear goals so you have a manageable task for each day and know exactly what you're doing. Then just focus on one small step at a time. When you manage your time this way, you don't need to spend hours at a time studying. Studying a small block of content for a short period each day helps you retain information better and avoid stressing over how much you have left to do. You can relax knowing that you have a plan to cover everything in time. In order for this strategy to be effective though, you have to start studying early and stick to your schedule. Avoid the exhaustion and futility that comes from last-minute cramming!

Study Environment

The environment you study in has a big impact on your learning. Studying in a coffee shop, while probably more enjoyable, is not likely to be as fruitful as studying in a quiet room. It's important to keep distractions to a minimum. You're only planning to study for a short block of time, so make the most of it. Don't pause to check your phone or get up to find a snack. It's also important to **avoid multitasking**. Research has consistently shown that multitasking will make your studying dramatically less effective. Your study area should also be comfortable and well-lit so you don't have the distraction of straining your eyes or sitting on an uncomfortable chair.

The time of day you study is also important. You want to be rested and alert. Don't wait until just before bedtime. Study when you'll be most likely to comprehend and remember. Even better, if you know what time of day your test will be, set that time aside for study. That way your brain will be used to working on that subject at that specific time and you'll have a better chance of recalling information.

Finally, it can be helpful to team up with others who are studying for the same test. Your actual studying should be done in as isolated an environment as possible, but the work of organizing the information and setting up the study plan can be divided up. In between study sessions, you can discuss with your teammates the concepts that you're all studying and quiz each other on the details. Just be sure that your teammates are as serious about the test as you are. If you find that your study time is being replaced with social time, you might need to find a new team.

Success Strategy #2 – Make Your Studying Count

You're devoting a lot of time and effort to preparing for this test, so you want to be absolutely certain it will pay off. This means doing more than just reading the content and hoping you can remember it on test day. It's important to make every minute of study count. There are two main areas you can focus on to make your studying count:

Retention

It doesn't matter how much time you study if you can't remember the material. You need to make sure you are retaining the concepts. To check your retention of the information you're learning, try recalling it at later times with minimal prompting. Try carrying around flashcards and glance at one or two from time to time or ask a friend who's also studying for the test to quiz you.

To enhance your retention, look for ways to put the information into practice so that you can apply it rather than simply recalling it. If you're using the information in practical ways, it will be much easier to remember. Similarly, it helps to solidify a concept in your mind if you're not only reading it to yourself but also explaining it to someone else. Ask a friend to let you teach them about a concept you're a little shaky on (or speak aloud to an imaginary audience if necessary). As you try to summarize, define, give examples, and answer your friend's questions, you'll understand the concepts better and they will stay with you longer. Finally, step back for a big picture view and ask yourself how each piece of information fits with the whole subject. When you link the different concepts together and see them working together as a whole, it's easier to remember the individual components.

Finally, practice showing your work on any multi-step problems, even if you're just studying. Writing out each step you take to solve a problem will help solidify the process in your mind, and you'll be more likely to remember it during the test.

Modality

Modality simply refers to the means or method by which you study. Choosing a study modality that fits your own individual learning style is crucial. No two people learn best in exactly the same way, so it's important to know your strengths and use them to your advantage.

For example, if you learn best by visualization, focus on visualizing a concept in your mind and draw an image or a diagram. Try color-coding your notes, illustrating them, or creating symbols that will trigger your mind to recall a learned concept. If you learn best by hearing or discussing information, find a study partner who learns the same way or read aloud to yourself. Think about how to put the information in your own words. Imagine that you are giving a lecture on the topic and record yourself so you can listen to it later.

For any learning style, flashcards can be helpful. Organize the information so you can take advantage of spare moments to review. Underline key words or phrases. Use different colors for different categories. Mnemonic devices (such as creating a short list in which every item starts with the same letter) can also help with retention. Find what works best for you and use it to store the information in your mind most effectively and easily.

Success Strategy #3 – Practice the Right Way

Your success on test day depends not only on how many hours you put into preparing, but also on whether you prepared the right way. It's good to check along the way to see if your studying is paying off. One of the most effective ways to do this is by taking practice tests to evaluate your progress. Practice tests are useful because they show exactly where you need to improve. Every time you take a practice test, pay special attention to these three groups of questions:

- The questions you got wrong
- The questions you had to guess on, even if you guessed right
- The questions you found difficult or slow to work through

This will show you exactly what your weak areas are, and where you need to devote more study time. Ask yourself why each of these questions gave you trouble. Was it because you didn't understand the material? Was it because you didn't remember the vocabulary? Do you need more repetitions on this type of question to build speed and confidence? Dig into those questions and figure out how you can strengthen your weak areas as you go back to review the material.

Additionally, many practice tests have a section explaining the answer choices. It can be tempting to read the explanation and think that you now have a good understanding of the concept. However, an explanation likely only covers part of the question's broader context. Even if the explanation makes sense, **go back and investigate** every concept related to the question until you're positive you have a thorough understanding.

As you go along, keep in mind that the practice test is just that: practice. Memorizing these questions and answers will not be very helpful on the actual test because it is unlikely to have any of the same exact questions. If you only know the right answers to the sample questions, you won't be prepared for the real thing. **Study the concepts** until you understand them fully, and then you'll be able to answer any question that shows up on the test.

It's important to wait on the practice tests until you're ready. If you take a test on your first day of study, you may be overwhelmed by the amount of material covered and how much you need to learn. Work up to it gradually.

On test day, you'll need to be prepared for answering questions, managing your time, and using the test-taking strategies you've learned. It's a lot to balance, like a mental marathon that will have a big impact on your future. Like training for a marathon, you'll need to start slowly and work your way up. When test day arrives, you'll be ready.

Start with what you've read in the first two Success Strategies—plan your course and study in the way that works best for you. If you have time, consider using multiple study resources to get different approaches to the same concepts. It can be helpful to see difficult concepts from more than one angle. Then find a good source for practice tests. Many times, the test website will suggest potential study resources or provide sample tests.

Practice Test Strategy

If you're able to find at least three practice tests, we recommend this strategy:

Untimed and Open-Book Practice

Take the first test with no time constraints and with your notes and study guide handy. Take your time and focus on applying the strategies you've learned.

Timed and Open-Book Practice

Take the second practice test open-book as well, but set a timer and practice pacing yourself to finish in time.

Timed and Closed-Book Practice

Take any other practice tests as if it were test day. Set a timer and put away your study materials. Sit at a table or desk in a quiet room, imagine yourself at the testing center, and answer questions as quickly and accurately as possible.

Keep repeating timed and closed-book tests on a regular basis until you run out of practice tests or it's time for the actual test. Your mind will be ready for the schedule and stress of test day, and you'll be able to focus on recalling the material you've learned.

Success Strategy #4 – Pace Yourself

Once you're fully prepared for the material on the test, your biggest challenge on test day will be managing your time. Just knowing that the clock is ticking can make you panic even if you have plenty of time left. Work on pacing yourself so you can build confidence against the time constraints of the exam. Pacing is a difficult skill to master, especially in a high-pressure environment, so **practice is vital**.

Set time expectations for your pace based on how much time is available. For example, if a section has 60 questions and the time limit is 30 minutes, you know you have to average 30 seconds or less per question in order to answer them all. Although 30 seconds is the hard limit, set 25 seconds per question as your goal, so you reserve extra time to spend on harder questions. When you budget extra time for the harder questions, you no longer have any reason to stress when those questions take longer to answer.

Don't let this time expectation distract you from working through the test at a calm, steady pace, but keep it in mind so you don't spend too much time on any one question. Recognize that taking extra time on one question you don't understand may keep you from answering two that you do understand later in the test. If your time limit for a question is up and you're still not sure of the answer, mark it and move on, and come back to it later if the time and the test format allow. If the testing format doesn't allow you to return to earlier questions, just make an educated guess; then put it out of your mind and move on.

On the easier questions, be careful not to rush. It may seem wise to hurry through them so you have more time for the challenging ones, but it's not worth missing one if you know the concept and just didn't take the time to read the question fully. Work efficiently but make sure you understand the question and have looked at all of the answer choices, since more than one may seem right at first.

Even if you're paying attention to the time, you may find yourself a little behind at some point. You should speed up to get back on track, but do so wisely. Don't panic; just take a few seconds less on each question until you're caught up. Don't guess without thinking, but do look through the answer choices and eliminate any you know are wrong. If you can get down to two choices, it is often worthwhile to guess from those. Once you've chosen an answer, move on and don't dwell on any that you skipped or had to hurry through. If a question was taking too long, chances are it was one of the harder ones, so you weren't as likely to get it right anyway.

On the other hand, if you find yourself getting ahead of schedule, it may be beneficial to slow down a little. The more quickly you work, the more likely you are to make a careless mistake that will affect your score. You've budgeted time for each question, so don't be afraid to spend that time. Practice an efficient but careful pace to get the most out of the time you have.

Test-Taking Strategies

This section contains a list of test-taking strategies that you may find helpful as you work through the test. By taking what you know and applying logical thought, you can maximize your chances of answering any question correctly!

It is very important to realize that every question is different and every person is different: no single strategy will work on every question, and no single strategy will work for every person. That's why we've included all of them here, so you can try them out and determine which ones work best for different types of questions and which ones work best for you.

Question Strategies

Read Carefully

Read the question and answer choices carefully. Don't miss the question because you misread the terms. You have plenty of time to read each question thoroughly and make sure you understand what is being asked. Yet a happy medium must be attained, so don't waste too much time. You must read carefully, but efficiently.

Contextual Clues

Look for contextual clues. If the question includes a word you are not familiar with, look at the immediate context for some indication of what the word might mean. Contextual clues can often give you all the information you need to decipher the meaning of an unfamiliar word. Even if you can't determine the meaning, you may be able to narrow down the possibilities enough to make a solid guess at the answer to the question.

Prefixes

If you're having trouble with a word in the question or answer choices, try dissecting it. Take advantage of every clue that the word might include. Prefixes and suffixes can be a huge help. Usually they allow you to determine a basic meaning. Pre- means before, post- means after, pro - is positive, de- is negative. From prefixes and suffixes, you can get an idea of the general meaning of the word and try to put it into context.

Hedge Words

Watch out for critical hedge words, such as *likely, may, can, sometimes, often, almost, mostly, usually, generally, rarely,* and *sometimes.* Question writers insert these hedge phrases to cover every possibility. Often an answer choice will be wrong simply because it leaves no room for exception. Be on guard for answer choices that have definitive words such as *exactly* and *always.*

Switchback Words

Stay alert for *switchbacks.* These are the words and phrases frequently used to alert you to shifts in thought. The most common switchback words are *but, although,* and *however.* Others include *nevertheless, on the other hand, even though, while, in spite of, despite, regardless of.* Switchback words are important to catch because they can change the direction of the question or an answer choice.

Face Value

When in doubt, use common sense. Accept the situation in the problem at face value. Don't read too much into it. These problems will not require you to make wild assumptions. If you have to go beyond creativity and warp time or space in order to have an answer choice fit the question, then you should move on and consider the other answer choices. These are normal problems rooted in reality. The applicable relationship or explanation may not be readily apparent, but it is there for you to figure out. Use your common sense to interpret anything that isn't clear.

Answer Choice Strategies

Answer Selection

The most thorough way to pick an answer choice is to identify and eliminate wrong answers until only one is left, then confirm it is the correct answer. Sometimes an answer choice may immediately seem right, but be careful. The test writers will usually put more than one reasonable answer choice on each question, so take a second to read all of them and make sure that the other choices are not equally obvious. As long as you have time left, it is better to read every answer choice than to pick the first one that looks right without checking the others.

Answer Choice Families

An answer choice family consists of two (in rare cases, three) answer choices that are very similar in construction and cannot all be true at the same time. If you see two answer choices that are direct opposites or parallels, one of them is usually the correct answer. For instance, if one answer choice says that quantity x increases and another either says that quantity x decreases (opposite) or says that quantity y increases (parallel), then those answer choices would fall into the same family. An answer choice that doesn't match the construction of the answer choice family is more likely to be incorrect. Most questions will not have answer choice families, but when they do appear, you should be prepared to recognize them.

Eliminate Answers

Eliminate answer choices as soon as you realize they are wrong, but make sure you consider all possibilities. If you are eliminating answer choices and realize that the last one you are left with is also wrong, don't panic. Start over and consider each choice again. There may be something you missed the first time that you will realize on the second pass.

Avoid Fact Traps

Don't be distracted by an answer choice that is factually true but doesn't answer the question. You are looking for the choice that answers the question. Stay focused on what the question is asking for so you don't accidentally pick an answer that is true but incorrect. Always go back to the question and make sure the answer choice you've selected actually answers the question and is not merely a true statement.

Extreme Statements

In general, you should avoid answers that put forth extreme actions as standard practice or proclaim controversial ideas as established fact. An answer choice that states the "process should be used in certain situations, if..." is much more likely to be correct than one that states the "process should be discontinued completely." The first is a calm rational statement and doesn't even make a definitive, uncompromising stance, using a hedge word *if* to provide wiggle room, whereas the second choice is a radical idea and far more extreme.

Benchmark

As you read through the answer choices and you come across one that seems to answer the question well, mentally select that answer choice. This is not your final answer, but it's the one that will help you evaluate the other answer choices. The one that you selected is your benchmark or standard for judging each of the other answer choices. Every other answer choice must be compared to your benchmark. That choice is correct until proven otherwise by another answer choice beating it. If you find a better answer, then that one becomes your new benchmark. Once you've decided that no other choice answers the question as well as your benchmark, you have your final answer.

Predict the Answer

Before you even start looking at the answer choices, it is often best to try to predict the answer. When you come up with the answer on your own, it is easier to avoid distractions and traps because you will know exactly what to look for. The right answer choice is unlikely to be word-for-word what you came up with, but it should be a close match. Even if you are confident that you have the right answer, you should still take the time to read each option before moving on.

General Strategies

Tough Questions

If you are stumped on a problem or it appears too hard or too difficult, don't waste time. Move on! Remember though, if you can quickly check for obviously incorrect answer choices, your chances of guessing correctly are greatly improved. Before you completely give up, at least try to knock out a couple of possible answers. Eliminate what you can and then guess at the remaining answer choices before moving on.

Check Your Work

Since you will probably not know every term listed and the answer to every question, it is important that you get credit for the ones that you do know. Don't miss any questions through careless mistakes. If at all possible, try to take a second to look back over your answer selection and make sure you've selected the correct answer choice and haven't made a costly careless mistake (such as marking an answer choice that you didn't mean to mark). This quick double check should more than pay for itself in caught mistakes for the time it costs.

Pace Yourself

It's easy to be overwhelmed when you're looking at a page full of questions; your mind is confused and full of random thoughts, and the clock is ticking down faster than you would like. Calm down and maintain the pace that you have set for yourself. Especially as you get down to the last few minutes of the test, don't let the small numbers on the clock make you panic. As long as you are on track by monitoring your pace, you are guaranteed to have time for each question.

Don't Rush

It is very easy to make errors when you are in a hurry. Maintaining a fast pace in answering questions is pointless if it makes you miss questions that you would have gotten right otherwise. Test writers like to include distracting information and wrong answers that seem right. Taking a little extra time to avoid careless mistakes can make all the difference in your test score. Find a pace that allows you to be confident in the answers that you select.

Keep Moving

Panicking will not help you pass the test, so do your best to stay calm and keep moving. Taking deep breaths and going through the answer elimination steps you practiced can help to break through a stress barrier and keep your pace.

Final Notes

The combination of a solid foundation of content knowledge and the confidence that comes from practicing your plan for applying that knowledge is the key to maximizing your performance on test day. As your foundation of content knowledge is built up and strengthened, you'll find that the strategies included in this chapter become more and more effective in helping you quickly sift through the distractions and traps of the test to isolate the correct answer.

Now it's time to move on to the test content chapters of this book, but be sure to keep your goal in mind. As you read, think about how you will be able to apply this information on the test. If you've already seen sample questions for the test and you have an idea of the question format and style, try to come up with questions of your own that you can answer based on what you're reading. This will give you valuable practice applying your knowledge in the same ways you can expect to on test day.

Good luck and good studying!

Real and Complex Number System

Real, natural, whole, integer, rational, irrational, imaginary, and complex numbers

The set of real numbers contains all numbers which have distinct locations on a number line. Natural numbers are real numbers used for counting: 1, 2, 3, 4, ... The set of whole numbers includes the counting numbers along with the number zero: 0, 1, 2, 3, 4, ... The set of integers includes whole numbers and their opposites: ..., -4, -3, -2, -1, 0, 1, 2, 3, 4, ... Rational numbers include any real number which can be expressed as a fraction in which the numerator is an integer and the denominator is a non-zero integer; rational numbers include integers, fractions, terminating, and repeating decimals. Irrational numbers, such as $\sqrt{2}$ and π, are real numbers which are not rational; in decimal form, these numbers are non-repeating and non-terminating, so any decimal (or fractional) representations of irrational numbers are only approximations. The set of imaginary numbers includes all numbers whose squares are negative and therefore excludes any real number; the imaginary number i is defined as the square root of -1. The set of complex numbers encompasses both the real and imaginary; a complex number can be written in the form $a + bi$, where a and b are real numbers, and i is the imaginary number.

Below is an example of a diagram which shows that natural numbers are a subset of whole numbers, which are a subset of integers, which are a subset of rational numbers. All of these together with irrational numbers comprise the set of real numbers. Complex numbers include both real and imaginary numbers.

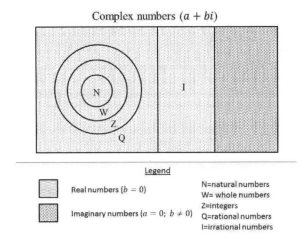

Complex numbers $(a + bi)$

Legend

Real numbers $(b = 0)$

Imaginary numbers $(a = 0;\ b \neq 0)$

N=natural numbers
W= whole numbers
Z=integers
Q=rational numbers
I=irrational numbers

Note that the sizes of the boxes and circles do not reflect the sizes of each set. Each set contains an infinite number of elements.

Example problems

Problem 1: Classify each of the following numbers as areal, natural, whole, integer, rational, irrational, imaginary, and/or complex.

$$\pi$$
$$-6$$
$$22$$
$$i$$
$$\frac{2}{3}$$
$$2 + 3i$$

π is an irrational number, a real number, and a complex number

-6 is an integer, a rational number, a real number, and a complex number

22 is a natural number, a whole number, an integer, a rational number, a real number, and a complex number

i is an imaginary number and a complex number

$\frac{2}{3}$ is a rational number, a real number, and a complex number

2+3i is a complex number

Problem 2: Determine whether each statement is true.

All natural numbers are real numbers.

Some integers are whole numbers.

Imaginary numbers are not real.

No integer is irrational.

All rational numbers are integers.

1. True; all natural numbers are real numbers.
2. True; some integers are whole numbers. Not all integers, however, are whole numbers, but all whole numbers are integers.
3. True; imaginary numbers are not real.
4. True; no integer is irrational. Integers are part of the set of rational numbers, and irrational numbers are not rational.
5. False; all rational numbers are NOT integers. All integers are rational, but not all rational numbers are integers.

- 13 -

$$(2 + 3i) + (6 - 2i) = 8 + i$$

$$(2 + 3i) - (6 - 2i) = -4 + 5i$$

$$(2 + 3i)(6 - 2i) = 12 - 4i + 18i - 6i^2 = 12 + 14i + 6 = 18 + 14i$$

Problem 5

Simplify $3i(2 + 4i) - (6 + 2i)^2$.

The commutative, associative, and distributive properties are true for complex numbers. Complex expressions can be simplified just as real, variable expressions are simplified. Keep in mind, however, that i is not a variable but is rather the imaginary number, so be sure to simplify i^2 to -1.

$$3i(2 + 4i) - (6 + 2i)^2$$

$$6i + 12i^2 - (36 + 24i + 4i^2)$$

$$6i + 12i^2 - 36 - 24i - 4i^2$$

$$-18i + 8i^2 - 36$$

$$-18i - 8 - 36$$

$$-44 - 18i$$

Problem 6

Graph these numbers on the complex plane.

$$-4$$

$$2i$$

$$3 - i$$

The complex plane is created by the intersection of a real, horizontal axis and an imaginary, vertical axis. For a complex number written in the form $a + bi$, a represents the displacement along the real axis and b along the imaginary axis. The number -4 is graphed in its appropriate position on the real number line, while $2i$ is graphed on the imaginary axis since its real number component a is 0. The complex number $3 - i$ is represented by a point on the plane which is three units to the right of the origin and one unit down.

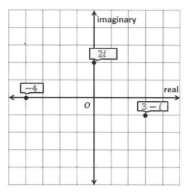

Modulus and conjugate of a complex number

The modulus, or absolute value, of a complex number $z = a + bi$ is the distance from the origin to point z graphed on the complex plane. Since that distance can be represented by the hypotenuse of a right triangle with leg lengths a and b, $|z|=\sqrt{a^2 + b^2}$.

The modulus of a complex number is always a real number.

The modulus of a complex number is always positive.

The modulus of a complex number is always a real number and is always positive. Since a and b represent real numbers, their squares are always positive, real numbers. The sum of two positive, real numbers must also be positive and real, so $a^2 + b^2$ is a positive, real quantity. The square root of a positive, real number is also a positive, real number, so $\sqrt{a^2 + b^2}$ must return a number that is both real and positive.

The conjugate of a complex number $a + bi$ is $a - bi$. The product of a complex number and its conjugate is always real:

$(a + bi)(a - bi) = a^2 - abi + abi - b^2i^2 = a^2 + b^2$. Since a and b are real, and since squares and sums of real numbers are also real, $a^2 + b^2$ is always real.

Example problems

Problem 1: Find the modulus and the conjugate of the complex number $4 + 3i$.

> The modulus, or absolute value, of a complex number is the number's distance from the origin when graphed on the complex plane. By graphing $4 + 3i$ on the complex plane, it is easy to see that its distance from the origin is the hypotenuse of a right triangle with leg lengths 4 and 3. Recognize 3-4-5 as a common Pythagorean triple,

or evaluate and simply the expression $\sqrt{a^2 + b^2}$, where $a = 4$ and $b = 3$:
$\sqrt{4^2 + 3^2} = \sqrt{16 + 9} = \sqrt{25} = 5$. So, the modulus of $4 + 3i$ is 5.

The conjugate of complex number $a + bi$ is defined as $a - bi$, so the conjugate of $4 + 3i$ is $4 - 3i$.

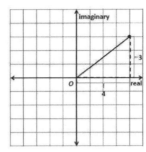

Problem 2: Write an equation which relates complex number z, its conjugate $\bar{z}$, and its modulus $|z|$.

Let $z = a + bi$. By definition, $\bar{z} = a - bi$, and $|z| = \sqrt{a^2 + b^2}$.

Since $z \cdot \bar{z} = (a + bi)(a - bi) = a^2 - abi + abi - b^2i^2 = a^2 + b^2$, and since $|z|^2 = \left(\sqrt{a^2 + b^2}\right)^2 = a^2 + b^2$, we have the relationship $\mathbf{z \cdot \bar{z} = |z|^2}$.

Problem 3: Use the property $z \cdot \bar{z} = |z|^2$, where z is a complex number and $\bar{z}$ and $|z|$ are its conjugate and modulus, respectively, to find the modulus of $3 + 4i$.

When $z = 3 + 4i, \bar{z} = 3 - 4i$.

$$|z|^2 = z \cdot \bar{z} = (3 + 4i)(3 - 4i) = 9 - 16i^2 = 25$$

$$|z| = 5$$

The modulus is representing the distance of a complex number from zero on the complex plane and can therefore not be negative. So, the modulus of $3 + 4i$ is 5.

Simplifying the quotient of two complex numbers

Example problems

Problem 1: Simplify $\frac{2-4i}{1+3i}$.

To simplify the quotient of two complex numbers, multiply the numerator and denominator by the complex conjugate of the denominator.

$$\frac{2 - 4i}{1 + 3i} = \frac{2 - 4i}{1 + 3i} \cdot \frac{1 - 3i}{1 - 3i} = \frac{2 - 6i - 4i + 12i^2}{1 - 9i^2} = \frac{2 - 10i - 12}{1 + 9} = \frac{-10 - 10i}{10}$$
$$= -1 - i$$

Problem 2: Simplify $\frac{3-i\sqrt{2}}{3+i\sqrt{2}}$.

To simplify the quotient of two complex numbers, multiply the numerator and denominator by the complex conjugate of the denominator.

- 18 -

$$\frac{3-i\sqrt{2}}{3+i\sqrt{2}} = \frac{3-i\sqrt{2}}{3+i\sqrt{2}} \cdot \frac{3-i\sqrt{2}}{3-i\sqrt{2}} = \frac{9-6i\sqrt{2}+2i^2}{9-2i^2} = \frac{9-6i\sqrt{2}-2}{9+2} = \frac{7-6i\sqrt{2}}{11}$$
$$= \frac{7}{11} - \frac{6\sqrt{2}}{11}i$$

Zero exponent property and negative exponent property

The zero exponent property states $a^0 = 1$ for all $a \neq 0$. The negative exponent property states $a^{-b} = \frac{1}{a^b}$ for all $a \neq 0$.

Consider the series ..., 2, 4, 8, 16, 32, ... Notice that each number is two times the previous number, so the series can be written ..., 2, $2 \cdot 2$,$2 \cdot 2 \cdot 2$, $2 \cdot 2 \cdot 2 \cdot 2$,$2 \cdot 2 \cdot 2 \cdot 2$, ..., which can be more easily expressed using powers of 2: ..., $2^1, 2^2, 2^3, 2^4, 2^5$, ... The exponent of each number is one more than the exponent of the previous number.

Extend the series a few numbers to the left: ..., $\frac{1}{4}$, $\frac{1}{2}$, 1, 2, 4, 8, 16, 32, ... Also, apply the pattern of exponents to the series written as powers of two: ..., 2^{-2}, 2^{-1}, $2^0, 2^1, 2^2, 2^3, 2^4, 2^5$, ... Compare the relative positions of newly written terms: $2^0 = 1$; $2^{-1} = \frac{1}{2} = \frac{1}{2^1}$; $2^{-2} = \frac{1}{4} = \frac{1}{2^2}$.

Product of powers property and quotient of powers property

The product of powers property states that when multiplying two monomials with like bases, add together the powers of that base; for example, $x^7 \cdot x^3 = x^{7+3} = x^{10}$ because $(x \cdot x \cdot x \cdot x \cdot x \cdot x \cdot x) \cdot (x \cdot x \cdot x) = x \cdot x \cdot x \cdot x \cdot x \cdot x \cdot x \cdot x \cdot x \cdot x = x^{10}$. The quotient of powers property states that when dividing two monomials with like bases, subtract the powers of that base; for example $\frac{x^7}{x^3} = x^{7-3} = x^4$ because $\frac{x \cdot x \cdot x \cdot x \cdot x \cdot x \cdot x}{x \cdot x \cdot x} = \frac{x}{x} \cdot \frac{x}{x} \cdot \frac{x}{x} \cdot x \cdot x \cdot x \cdot x = 1 \cdot 1 \cdot 1 \cdot x \cdot x \cdot x \cdot x = x^4$.

Power of a product, power of a quotient, and power of a power

The power of a product property states that when multiplying together two monomials with the same power but different bases, multiply the bases and keep the power the same; for example, $x^3 \cdot y^3 = (xy)^3$ because $x^3 \cdot y^3 = x \cdot x \cdot x \cdot y \cdot y \cdot y = x \cdot y \cdot x \cdot y \cdot x \cdot y = (x \cdot y) \cdot (x \cdot y) \cdot (x \cdot y) = (xy)^3$. (Notice the use of the commutative and associate properties of multiplication.) Similarly, the power of a quotient property states that when diving two monomials with the same power but different bases, divide the bases and keep the power the same; for example, $\frac{x^3}{y^3} = \left(\frac{x}{y}\right)^3$ because, $\frac{x^3}{y^3} = \frac{x \cdot x \cdot x}{y \cdot y \cdot y} = \frac{x}{y} \cdot \frac{x}{y} \cdot \frac{x}{y} = \left(\frac{x}{y}\right)^3$. Lastly, the power of a power property states that when raising a monomial to a power, multiply the power of each term in the monomial by the power to which the monomial is raised; for example, $(x^3 y^2)^3 = x^{3 \cdot 3} y^{2 \cdot 3} = x^9 y^6$ because $(x^3 y^2)^3 = (x \cdot x \cdot x \cdot y \cdot y)(x \cdot x \cdot x \cdot y \cdot y)(x \cdot x \cdot x \cdot y \cdot y) = x \cdot x \cdot x \cdot x \cdot x \cdot x \cdot x \cdot x \cdot x \cdot y \cdot y \cdot y \cdot y \cdot y \cdot y = x^9 y^6$ (Again, notice the use of the commutative and associate properties of multiplication.).

$$\sqrt[n]{x} = x^{\frac{1}{n}}$$

Below is an example illustrating $\sqrt[n]{x} = x^{\frac{1}{n}}$.

$$\sqrt{3} = 3^{\frac{1}{2}}$$

- 19 -

In this example, $x = 3$ and $n = 2$.

$\left(\sqrt{3}\right)^2 = \left(3^{\frac{1}{2}}\right)^2$ The inverse operation of taking the square root is raising to the second power. Perform the same operation on both sides of the equation.

$$3 = 3^{\frac{1}{2}\cdot 2}$$

To raise a power to a power, multiply the powers.

$$3 = 3^1$$

Simplify. $\frac{1}{2}\cdot 2 = 1$.

$$3=3$$

Simplify. $3^{\wedge}1 = 3$.

Integers and rational numbers closed under certain operations

When two integers are added, subtracted, or multiplied, the resulting sum, difference, or product is also an integer; therefore, the set of integers is closed under these operations. Given that a, b, c, and d are integers and that b and d do not equal zero,

$$\frac{a}{b}+\frac{c}{d} = \frac{ad+bc}{bd} \text{ and } \frac{a}{b}-\frac{c}{d} = \frac{ad-bc}{bd} \text{ and } \frac{a}{b}\cdot\frac{c}{d} = \frac{ac}{bd}$$

$\frac{a}{b}$ and $\frac{c}{d}$ are rational numbers. The products ad, bc, and bd are integers since the product of two integers is always an integer; likewise, since the sum or difference of two integers is always an integer, $ad + bc$ and $ad - bc$ must also be integers. Therefore, $\frac{ad+bc}{bd}$, $\frac{ad-bc}{bd}$, and $\frac{ac}{bd}$ represent ratios of two integers and are, by definition, rational. So, the set of rational numbers is closed under addition, subtraction, and multiplication.

Example problems

Problem 1

Simplify the expression $\sqrt[6]{9x^4}$.

$\left(9x^4\right)^{\frac{1}{6}}$ Rewrite the expression using rational exponents

$$\left(3^2 x^4\right)^{\frac{1}{6}}$$

Substitute 3^2 for 9.

$$3^{\frac{1}{3}}x^{\frac{2}{3}}$$

Use the power of a power property of exponents.

$$3^{\frac{1}{3}}x^{\frac{1}{3}}x^{\frac{1}{3}}$$

- 20 -

Use the product of a power property to rewrite $x^{\frac{2}{3}}$ as the product of $x^{\frac{1}{3}}$ and $x^{\frac{1}{3}}$.

$$(3xx)^{\frac{1}{3}}$$

Use the product of powers property to rewrite the expression

$$\sqrt[3]{3x^2}$$

Simplify.

Problem 2

Determine if the following statements are true or false. Provide an explanation for the true statement(s) and a counterexample for the false statement(s).

The sum of a rational number and an irrational number is always irrational.

The sum of two irrational numbers is always irrational.

1. It is true that the sum of a rational number and an irrational number is always irrational. Consider for a moment that the statement is false; this would require the existence of some irrational number x that when added to rational number a would produce rational number b: $a + x = b$. Solving the equation for x yields $x = b - a$. The difference of b and a must be rational since the set of rational numbers is closed under subtraction. Since $x = b - a$, x must be a rational number; there is no such irrational number x that when added to a rational number yields a rational number. Therefore, the sum of a rational and an irrational number is always irrational.
2. It is false that the sum of two irrational numbers is always irrational. For example, the sum of irrational numbers $\sqrt{3}$ and $-\sqrt{3}$ is zero, which is rational.

Problem 3

Determine if the following statements are true or false. Provide an explanation for true statements and a counterexample for false statements.

The product of a nonzero rational number and an irrational number is always irrational.

The product of two irrational numbers is always irrational.

1. It is true that the product of a nonzero rational number and an irrational number is always irrational. Consider for a moment that the statement is false; this would require the existence of some irrational number x that when multiplied by rational number a would produce rational number b: $ax = b$. Solving the equation for x yields $x = \frac{b}{a}$; $a \neq 0$. If x is equal to the ratio of two rational numbers, it must also, by definition, be rational. (Note that the ratio of two rational numbers can be rewritten as the ratio of two integers.) So, there is no such irrational number x that when multiplied by a rational number yields a rational number. Therefore, the product of a rational and an irrational number is irrational.
2. It is false that the product of two irrational numbers is always irrational. For example, the product of irrational numbers $\sqrt{3}$ and $-\sqrt{3}$ is -3, which is rational.

Determine if the following statement is always true, sometimes true, or never true: an integer raised to a non-integer power is an integer.

It is sometimes true that an integer raised to a non-integer power is an integer. For example, $4^{\frac{1}{2}} = \sqrt{4} = 2$. However, it is not always true. For example, $3^{\frac{1}{2}} = \sqrt{3}$.

Relations and Functions

Domain and range

If we think of a function as a procedure that takes a given input and produces a given output, the domain of the function is the set of all permissible inputs and the range is the set of all possible outputs. In other words, any value that we could "plug in" to the function and get a meaningful answer is in the domain of the function, and the answer we would get if we plugged in that value would be in the range of the function. When we plot a function on the xy-coordinate plane, the domain is the set of all x-values covered by the function, and the range is the set of all the *y*-values.

Scatter plot

Any collection of data points can be displayed as a scatter plot simply by graphing each of the points on a coordinate grid. The resulting graph will be a set of unconnected points rather than a line or curve. However, a line or curve can be found that fits the points approximately, if not exactly. The line or curve of "best fit" can then be used to predict other data points; we simply assume that these data points will lie directly on the line or curve, and use the equation of the line or curve to predict the *y*-value that will result from each *x*-value.

Graphs of functions

The graph of a linear function is a straight line.

The graph of a quadratic function is a parabola.

The graph of an exponential function increases more and more rapidly as it moves from left to right, and has a horizontal asymptote at y = 0.

A logarithmic function is the inverse of an exponential function. Its graph has a vertical asymptote at x = 0, and increases less rapidly as it moves from left to right.

The graph of an absolute value function is like a linear function, but with the negative portion of the graph reflected back across the *x*-axis.

The graph of a square root function is the upper half of a parabola lying on its side.

The graph of a rational function consists of two branches, one in the first quadrant and one in the third quadrant. Each branch decreases from left to right and has asymptotes at x = 0 and y = 0.

Changing constants in equations

Linear equations

Changing the constants *m* and *b* in a linear equation of the form y = mx + b affects the graph of the function. The constant *m* represents the slope of the graph. If *m* is positive, the graph slopes upward from left to right; if *m* is negative, the graph slopes downward. The greater the absolute value of *m*, the steeper the slope of the graph. The constant *b* represents the *y*-intercept of the graph, but it also represents how far and in what direction the graph has been shifted vertically compared to the base function $y = mx$. Increasing b shifts the graph upward and decreasing b shifts it downward, while the slope of the graph remains the same.

Quadratic equations

Changing the constants a and c in a quadratic equation of the form $y = ax^2 + bx + c$ affects the graph of the function. The x^2-coefficient a determines the width of the parabola described by the equation. A higher value of a means that the parabola slopes upward more steeply, and is therefore narrower. A lower value results in a wider, shallower parabola. Furthermore, a positive value of a means that the parabola is concave up, and a negative value means it is concave down. The constant term c represents a vertical shift of the parabola. Increasing the value of c shifts the parabola upward, and decreasing c shifts it downward. If $c = 0$, the parabola passes through the origin (though its vertex is not necessarily at the origin).

Exponential equations

Changing the constant a in an exponential equation of the form $y = a^x$ affects the graph of the function. The orientation of an exponential function graph depends on the magnitude and sign of the base a. If a is positive, the graph lies above the x-axis; if a is negative, the graph lies below the x-axis. If the absolute value of a is greater than 1, the graph approaches the x-axis as it moves to the left and approaches infinity as it moves to the right; if the absolute value of a is less than 1, the graph approaches the x-axis as it moves to the right and approaches infinity as it moves to the left; and if the absolute value of a equals 1, the graph is simply a horizontal line. Furthermore, the graph slopes more steeply upward or downward the farther a is from 1.

Graph of a function and graph of its inverse

The inverse of a function is the same as the original function, only with the independent and dependent variables switched. In other words, the inverse is what results if we take the original function and replace the x's with y's and the y's with x's. Hence, the graph of the inverse function looks the same as the graph of the original function would look if the x-axis and y-axis were exchanged. To swap the positive x-axis with the positive y-axis and the negative x-axis with the negative y-axis, it is necessary to flip the entire coordinate plane about the line $y = x$. Therefore, the graph of the inverse function is simply the graph of the original function flipped about the line $y = x$.

Consistent, inconsistent, and dependent systems of equations

A consistent system of equations has exactly one solution; that is, there is exactly one ordered pair that is a solution to both equations. The graphs of the two equations are lines that intersect at exactly one point.

An inconsistent system has no solutions. The graphs of the two equations are parallel lines.

A dependent system has infinitely many solutions; that is, every ordered pair that is a solution to one equation is a solution to the other equation as well. The graphs of the two equations are both graphs of the same line.

Substitution and elimination for solving linear systems

To solve a linear system by substitution, we rearrange one of the equations to isolate one variable. This tells us what expression to substitute for that variable in the other equation.

For example, given the system:

$$x + 3y = 5$$

$$2x - 4y = 3$$

We can rewrite the first equation as x = 5 – 3y. Then we can rewrite the second equation as 2(5 – 3y) – 4y = 3, and solve for y.

To solve a system by elimination, we add multiples of the two equations together in such a way that one variable drops out; then we solve for the remaining variable.

For example, to solve the system given above, we could multiply the first equation by -2, giving us:

$$-2x - 6y = -10$$

$$2x - 4y = 3$$

Adding the two equations together yields 0x – 10y = -7, or simply -10y = -7, which we can then solve for y.

Relationship between the functions y = a^x and y = log$_a$ x

The functions y = a^x and y = log$_a$ x are inverses of each other; that is, for any two numbers p and q, if p = a^q then q = log$_a$ p. Consequently, applying both functions in succession gives us the original input back again; that is, log$_a$(a^x) = x, and $a^{\log_a x} = x$.

Since the two functions are inverses, their graphs are identical to each other, but flipped about the line y = x. Where the exponential graph has a horizontal asymptote, the logarithmic graph has a vertical asymptote; where the exponential graph slopes more steeply as it moves to the right (or left), the logarithmic graph slopes less steeply.

Terms in the exponential growth formula x(t) = x$_0$ · e^{kt}

x(t) represents the value of the dependent variable x as a function of time (Note that x is the dependent variable here, although we usually see it as the independent variable.) x_0 represents the value of x at time t = 0, which is whatever time we begin measuring. t is the amount of time that has passed since t = 0, and k is the constant of exponential growth. The specific value of k depends on the specific situation being modeled, and a negative value of k indicates that exponential decay, rather than growth, is occurring.

Example problems

Problem 1

State the domain and range of the function y = x^2 + 5.

> The domain of the function is the set of all permissible x-values—in other words, all x-values that will yield a real y-value when plugged into the function. Any real number will yield a real number when squared, so the set of permissible values for x is the set of all real numbers.

> The range of the function is the set of all possible y-values the function can attain. There is a limit to the range of this function: if x is a real number, the value of x^2 can

- 25 -

never be less than zero. Therefore, the value of $x^2 + 5$ can never be less than 5, so the range of the function is the set of all real numbers greater than or equal to 5.

Problem 2

Mariel has ten coins in her pocket. All of them are quarters and dimes, and their total value is $1.60. How many of each type of coin does she have?

To solve this problem, we can set up a system of two linear equations. If Q is the number of quarters and D is the number of dimes, we have:

$$D + Q = 10$$

$$10D + 25Q = 160$$

This system is solved most easily by substitution. The first equation can be rewritten as $D = 10 - Q$, and then the expression $10 - Q$ can be substituted for D in the second equation, giving us $10(10 - Q) + 25Q = 160$. Solving:

$$10(10 - Q) + 25Q = 160$$

$$100 - 10Q + 25Q = 160$$

$$100 + 15Q = 160$$

$$15Q = 60$$

$$Q = 4$$

Mariel has 4 quarters.

Substituting 4 for Q in the first equation, we get $D + 4 = 10$, so $D = 6$. Mariel has 6 dimes.

Problem 3

State the domain and range of the function $y = 2\ln(x + 5)$.

The domain of the function $y = \ln x$ is the set of all positive real numbers, with a vertical exponent at $x = 0$. The range is the set of all real numbers.

Multiplying the natural log function by a constant does not affect the domain and range. However, adding a constant to the argument of the function does. The natural log function can only operate on positive numbers, but it operates on all positive numbers; therefore, the function $y = 2\ln(x + 5)$ exists for all values of x that make the quantity $(x + 5)$ greater than zero. That means that the domain of the function is the set of all real numbers greater than -5.

Problem 4

Solve the equation $2 \cdot (4)^x = (4)^{2x-2}$ for x. Does solving it become easier if we replace 4 with 2^2?

To solve the equation in its original form, first we take the $\log_4$ of both sides: $\log_4 (2 \cdot (4)^x) = \log_4 (4)^{2x-2}$. The left-hand side becomes $\log_4 (2) + \log_4 (4)^x$, or $0.5 + x$;

- 26 -

the right-hand side becomes simply $2x - 2$. So we have $x + 0.5 = 2x - 2$; subtracting x from both sides and adding 2 to both sides, we get $x = 2.5$.

Replacing 4 with 2^2 requires us to multiply exponents; we end up with $2 \cdot (2)^{2x} = (2)^{4x-4}$. However, now we can simplify the left-hand side to $(2)^{2x+1}$; then we can take the $\log_2$ of both sides without having to deal with square roots or fractional logarithms. We end up with $2x + 1 = 4x - 4$, or $2x = -5$, which once again gives us $x = 2.5$.

Problem 5

Solve the inequality $3(\ln x) + 4 < 10$ for x.

The first step is to get the logarithm isolated on one side of the inequality. Subtracting 4 from both sides and dividing by 3 gives us $\ln x < 2$. Then, raising e to the power of both sides yields $x < e^2$. This value can be approximated as 7.389, or left as it is.

However, we also must consider the limited domain of the natural log function: it is only defined for positive values of x. This means that the solution to our inequality is not simply the set of real numbers less than e^2; instead it is the set of real numbers greater than 0 and less than e^2.

Problem 6

Marshall puts $1000 in a savings account that earns 4% interest compounded annually. How many years will it take for him to have at least $1200 in the account?

The formula that determines how much money will be in the account after y years is $m = 1000 \cdot 1.04^y$. We want to find the value of y for which m will be at least 1200, so we set up the inequality $1200 \leq 1000 \cdot 1.04^y$ and solve it for y.

Dividing both sides by 1000 gives us $1.2 \leq 1.04^y$; we then take the $\log_{1.04}$ of both sides to get $\log_{1.04}(1.2) \leq y$. To find this logarithm, we can use the change of base property: $\log_{1.04}(1.2) = \frac{\ln 1.2}{\ln 1.04}$. Plugging this into a calculator, we get approximately 4.6.

Since interest is compounded once a year, we round up: it will take at least 5 years for Marshall to have $1200.

Extraneous solution

An extraneous solution is the solution of an equation that arises during the process of solving an equation, which is <u>not</u> a solution of the original equation. When solving a rational equation, each side is often multiplied by x or an expression containing x. Since the value of x is unknown, this may mean multiplying by zero, which will make any equation the true statement $0 = 0$. Similarly, when solving a radical expression, each side of the equation is often squared, or raised to some power. This can also change the sign of unknown expressions. For example, the equation $3 = -3$ is false, but squaring each side gives $9 = 9$, which is true.

- 27 -

General form of a complex number

The general form of a complex number is $a + bi$, where a and b are real numbers. The imaginary number i is equal to the square root of -1: $i = \sqrt{-1}$. Therefore the number i itself is a complex number, with $a = 0$ and $b = 1$. Other examples of complex numbers include $-12i$ and $\sqrt{3} + 4i$. Note that all real numbers are also complex numbers: if b = 0, then $a + bi = a + 0i = a$, which is a real number.

Graph of a linear system with no solution

If a linear system has no solution, there is no value of x and y that satisfies both equations of the system. Graphically, this means that the lines that represent each equation of the system will never intersect. Lines that never intersect are by definition parallel. Parallel lines have the same slope, so it can often be determined that a system has no solution without graphing or solving algebraically. For example, if the equations of the system are $y = -2x + 3$ and $y = -2x - 5$, the system has no solution. The equations represent distinct parallel lines.

Possible solutions for a system consisting of a linear and a quadratic equation

For a system that consists of a linear equation and a quadratic equation, it is possible to have 0, 1, or 2 solutions. This is different than a linear system, which has 0 solutions, 1 solutions, or infinitely many solutions. When a linear solution has infinitely many solutions, the two equations in the system are equivalent. A line may never intersect a parabola (0 solutions), or may be tangent to the parabola (1 solution), or may intersect the parabola in two points (2 solutions). Since solving a linear/quadratic system leads to a quadratic equation, it is not possible to have more than 2 solutions; that is, no line can intersect a parabola at more than 2 points.

Example problems

Problem 1

Solve $3x - 2 = -5$ by first assuming the solution exists. Explicitly justify each step.

> Assume that the solution exists, and that each side of the equation represents the same real number. In this case, that real number is
>
> -5, since the right side of the equation is -5. Adding 2 to each side results in two more equal numbers. So, the equation can be transformed as follows:
>
> $3x - 2 = -5$
>
> $3x - 2 + 2 = -5 + 2$
>
> $3x = -3$
>
> The same approach can be taken with the new equation. Since each side of the equation represents the same real number, divide each side by 3:

$$3x = -3$$

$$\frac{3x}{3} = \frac{-3}{3}$$

- 28 -

$$x = -1$$

The solution of the equation is $x = -1$.

Problem 2

Tom says the equation $3x = 5x$ has no solution. Explain his error.

Tom made an error, because the correct (and only) solution is $x = 0$. Tom may have incorrectly thought that 3 times a number can't possibly equal 5 times the same number, or perhaps he divided each side by the variable x. A correct method of solving the equation would be to assume there is a solution, so that each side equals the same real number. Subtract $3x$ from each side, yielding $0 = 2x$, each side of which equals some real number as well, since $3x$ was a real number. Dividing each side by 2 yields $x = 0$, which is the correct solution.

Problem 3

Find the solution of the equation $x^2 = 36$. Justify your solution method.

One method of solution is to assume there is a solution, so that x^2 and 36 each represent the same real number. Subtract 36 from each side, so that $x^2 - 36 = 0$. The expression on the left side can be factored, and the equation rewritten as $(x + 6)(x - 6) = 0$. If a product of two numbers is equal to zero, then one (or the other) of the numbers must be zero. This leads to the two equations $x + 6 = 0$ and $x - 6 = 0$. Assuming these equations have solutions, add (or subtract) 6 from each side to arrive at the two solutions, $x = -6$ or $x = 6$.

Problem 4

Solve $\frac{6}{x} = \frac{9}{10}$. Explain how each step follows from the equality of numbers.

Assume that the solution exists, and that $\frac{6}{x}$ and $\frac{9}{10}$ equal the same real number. Since $\frac{9}{10}$ is positive, and a positive number divided by a positive number is positive, the value of x must be positive. Multiply each side of the equation by x to get $6 = \frac{9x}{10}$, where each side again represents the same real number. Then multiply each side by $\frac{10}{9}$, to arrive at the solution $\frac{60}{9} = x$.

Problem 5

Solve the rational equation $\frac{2}{x} - 2 = x - 1$.

To solve the rational equation, multiply each side of the equation by the LCD, which is x. This will transform the rational equation into a quadratic equation that can be solved by factoring:

$$\frac{2}{x} - 2 = x - 1$$

$$x\left(\frac{2}{x} - 2\right) = x(x - 1)$$

- 29 -

$$2 - 2x = x^2 - x$$

$$x^2 + x - 2 = 0$$

$$(x + 2)(x - 1) = 0$$

$$x = -2, x = 1$$

Both $x = -2$ and $x = 1$ check out in the original equation. The solution is $x = \{-2, 1\}$.

Problem 6

Solve the radical equation $\sqrt{x - 1} + 3 = x$.

To solve the radical equation, isolate the radical $\sqrt{x - 1}$ on one side of the equation. Then square both sides and solve the resulting quadratic equation:

$$\sqrt{x - 1} + 3 = x$$

$$\sqrt{x - 1} = x - 3$$

$$\left(\sqrt{x - 1}\right)^2 = (x - 3)^2$$

$$x - 1 = x^2 - 6x + 9$$

$$x^2 - 7x + 10 = 0$$

$$(x - 5)(x - 2) = 0$$

$$x = 2, x = 5$$

Only $x = 5$ checks out in the original equation; $\sqrt{2 - 1} + 3 \overset{?}{\Leftrightarrow} 2 \xrightarrow{yields} \sqrt{1} + 3 = 4 \neq 2!$ The solution, then, is just $x = \{5\}$.

Problem 7

Solve $x + 1 = \sqrt{x + 1}$. Check for extraneous solutions.

To solve the radical equation, square both sides and solve the resulting quadratic equation by factoring:

$$x + 1 = \sqrt{x + 1}$$

$$(x + 1)^2 = \left(\sqrt{x + 1}\right)^2$$

$$x^2 + 2x + 1 = x + 1$$

$$x^2 + x = 0$$

$$x(x + 1) = 0$$

$$x = -1, x = 0$$

To check whether either solution is extraneous, substitute into the original equation:

$$x + 1 = \sqrt{x + 1}$$
$$-1 + 1 = \sqrt{-1 + 1}$$
$$0 = 0$$

$$x + 1 = \sqrt{x + 1}$$
$$0 + 1 = \sqrt{0 + 1}$$
$$0 = 0$$

Both solutions are valid. The solution is $x = \{-1, 0\}$.

Problem 8

Find the solution of the inequality $-4x + 2 \leq -10$.

To solve the inequality, isolate the variable x on one side. When multiplying or dividing by negative numbers, change the inequality symbol from $\leq$ to $\geq$, or vice versa:

$-4x + 2 \leq -10$

$-4x + 2 - 2 \leq -10 - 2$

$-4x \leq -12$

$$\frac{-4x}{-4} \geq \frac{-12}{-4}$$

$$x \geq 3$$

The solution of the inequality is $x \geq 3$. (Note that when $x = 3$, both sides of the inequality equal -10. Also, when $x = 4$, the inequality is $-14 \leq -10$, which is true. Therefore the solution is correct.)

Problem 9

A softball player's average is the number of hits divided by the number of at-bats. Gene currently has 20 hits in 75 at-bats. If he can get 30 more at-bats, how many hits must he get to have an average of 0.300 or better?

Let h represent the number of additional hits Gene gets in the 30 at-bats. His total number of hits will be 20 + h, and his total number of at-bats will be 75 + 30 = 105. The quotient of these two expressions represents Gene's average. Write a greater-than-or-equal-to inequality for this situation:

$$\frac{20 + h}{105} \geq 0.300$$

$$20 + h \geq 31.5$$

$$h \geq 11.5$$

Since there is no such thing as half a hit, Gene needs 12 or more hits in the next 30 at-bats to have an average of 0.300 or better.

Problem 10

A cab company charges $8 to enter the cab, and then $.42 per mile. If the ride cost $19.76, how long was the trip, in miles?

Let m represent the number of miles for a ride in the cab. The total cost is the $8 to enter the cab, plus $.42 per mile. If c represents the total cost for a ride of m miles, an equation for the total cost is

c = 8 + 0.42m. Substitute 19.76 for c in the equation and solve for

m: 8 + 0.42m = 19.76

0.42m = 11.76

$$\frac{0.42m}{0.42} = \frac{11.76}{0.42}$$

$$m = 28$$

A ride that cost $19.76 was 28 miles long.

Problem 11

Solve the linear equation $ax + b = c$, where a, b, and c are real numbers. State any restrictions on the values of a, b, and c.

The equation can be solved the same way as if the parameters a, b, and c were real numbers. Isolate x on one side of the equation:

$$ax + b = c$$

$$ax = c - b$$

- 32 -

$$\frac{ax}{a} = \frac{c-b}{a}$$

$$x = \frac{c-b}{a}$$

The solution is $x = \frac{c-b}{a}$. Since division by zero is undefined, the value of a must be nonzero. However, if the value of a were zero, the original equation would not be a one-variable equation, but would simply read $b = c$.

<u>Problem 12</u>

Rewrite $x^2 + 4x = 2$ in the form $(x - p)^2 = q$.

To rewrite $x^2 + 4x = 2$ in the form $(x - p)^2 = q$, complete the square. Begin by adding the square of one half the coefficient of x to each side. In this case, the coefficient is 4, so add $(\frac{1}{2} \cdot 4)^2 = 4$ to both sides, and rewrite the trinomial as a squared binomial:

$$x^2 + 4x = 2$$

$$x^2 + 4x + 4 = 2 + 4$$

$$x^2 + 4x + 4 = 6$$

$$(x + 2)^2 = 6$$

This equation is in the form $(x - p)^2 = q$, with $p = -2$ and $q = 6$.

<u>Problem 13</u>

Complete the square in the equation $3x^2 - 5x = 2$.

To complete the square, first divide by 3 so that the leading coefficient (the coefficient of x^2) is 1. Then add the square of one half the coefficient of x to each side of the equation, and rewrite the trinomial as a squared binomial:

$$3x^2 - 5x = 2$$

$$x^2 - \frac{5}{3}x = \frac{2}{3}$$

$$x^2 - \frac{5}{3}x + \left(\frac{5}{6}\right)^2 = 2 + \left(\frac{5}{6}\right)^2$$

$$x^2 - \frac{5}{3}x + \frac{25}{36} = \frac{72}{36} + \frac{25}{36} = \frac{97}{36}$$

$$\left(x + \frac{5}{6}\right)^2 = \frac{97}{36}$$

<u>Problem 14</u>

Derive the quadratic formula by completing the square in the general quadratic equation

- 33 -

$ax^2 + bx + c = 0.$

To derive the quadratic formula by completing the square, follow the steps below.

Starting at $ax^2 + bx + c = 0$, subtract c from both sides, then divide each term by a:

$$x^2 + \frac{b}{a}x = -\frac{c}{a}$$

Complete the square by adding $\left(\frac{1}{2} \cdot \frac{b}{a}\right)^2 = \frac{b^2}{4a^2}$ to both sides:

$$x^2 + \frac{b}{a}x + \frac{b^2}{4a^2} = \frac{b^2}{4a^2} - \frac{c}{a}$$

Rewrite the trinomial on the left side as a perfect square:

$$\left(x + \frac{b}{2a}\right)^2 = \frac{b^2}{4a^2} - \frac{c}{a}$$

Find the common denominator to subtract on the left; then take the square root of both sides:

$$x + \frac{b}{2a} = \pm\sqrt{\frac{b^2 - 4ac}{4a^2}}$$

Solve for x and simplify:

$$x = \frac{-b \pm \sqrt{b^2 - 4ac}}{2a}$$

Problem 15

Compare the quadratic forms $a(x - m)(x - n) = 0$ and $(x - p)^2 = q$. What are the solutions of each equation?

The quadratic equation $a(x - m)(x - n) = 0$ is in factored form. Since the right side of the equation is zero, the factors make it easy to find the solutions: the two equations $x - m = 0$ and $x - n = 0$ give the solutions $x = m$ and $x = n$. The equation $(x - p)^2 = q$ has the form of a quadratic after completing the square, which means the left side is a squared binomial. Taking the square root of each side and then adding p to each side of the equation gives the solutions $x = p \pm \sqrt{q}$.

Problem 16

Solve $4x^2 = 100$ by inspection.

To solve an equation by inspection means to solve using fairly obvious mental math, without performing calculations on paper or with a calculator. Dividing each side of the equation by 4 gives $x^2 = 25$. The two square roots of 25 are –5 and 5, so the solution of the equation is $x = -5$ or $x = 5$. A check of each solution (by substituting into the original equation) can seem self-evident:

$4x^2 = 100$	$4x^2 = 100$
$4(-5)^2 = 100$	$4(5)^2 = 100$
$4(25) = 100$	$4(25) = 100$
$100 = 100$	$100 = 100$

Problem 17

Write the quadratic formula. Apply it to solve the equation $2x^2 = 5x - 1$.

The quadratic formula is $x = \frac{-b \pm \sqrt{b^2 - 4ac}}{2a}$. It gives the solution of the quadratic equation $ax^2 + bx + c = 0$. The equation $2x^2 = 5x - 1$ can be written in this form as $2x^2 - 5x + 1 = 0$. Substitute into the quadratic formula with $a = 2$, $b = -5$, and $c = 1$:

$$x = \frac{-b \pm \sqrt{b^2 - 4ac}}{2a}$$

$$x = \frac{-(-5) \pm \sqrt{(-5)^2 - 4(2)(1)}}{2(2)}$$

$$x = \frac{5 \pm \sqrt{17}}{4}$$

The solutions of the equation are $x = \frac{5 + \sqrt{17}}{4}$ and $x = \frac{5 - \sqrt{17}}{4}$.

Problem 18

Bethany claims the solutions of $(x - 2)(x + 3) = -4$ are $x = -3$ and $x = 2$. Explain and correct her error.

Bethany applied the zero-product property to an equation that does not equal zero. Although her values of x make the left side of the equation zero, the right side is -4. To correct her error, she should first multiply the binomials, and then write the equation so that the right side is zero:

$(x - 2)(x + 3) = -4$

$x^2 - 2x + 3x - 6 = -4$

$x^2 + x - 6 = -4$

$x^2 + x - 2 = 0$

$(x + 2)(x - 1) = 0$

$x = -2$ or $x = 1$

The solution is $x = \{-2, 1\}$.

Problem 19

Without solving either system, explain why the systems below have the

same solution. Then verify this fact.

$\begin{cases} x + y = 4 \\ 2x - y = -1 \end{cases}$ $\qquad \begin{cases} x + y = 4 \\ 3x = 3 \end{cases}$

When comparing the two systems, it is clear that the first equation of each system is the same. If an equation of one system is a linear combination of the equations of the other system, then the systems are equivalent and therefore have the same solution. A linear combination is the sum of two equations, with either equation possibly multiplied by a real number. Adding the two equations of the first system results in the equation $3x = 3$. This is the 2nd equation of the other system, so the systems are equivalent and have the same solution. The solution is $(x, y) = (1, 3)$ and satisfies both systems.

Problem 20

Show that if (a, b) is the solution to the system on the left below, then it is also the solution to the system on the right. In the system on the right, one equation was replaced with the sum of that equation and a multiple of the first equation.

$\begin{cases} 3x + 8y = 2 \\ 2x - 5y = -7 \end{cases} \qquad \begin{cases} 3x + 8y = 2 \\ 3x + 8y + k(2x - 5y) = 2 - 7k \end{cases}$

The solution of the original system is (a, b). Substituting these values for x and y in the equations gives the following true statements:

$$3a + 8b = 2$$

- 36 -

$$2a - 5b = -7$$

To show that (a, b) is the solution of the system on the right, show that (a, b) makes both equations true. The first equation $3x + 8y = 2$ is true, because it is the same equation as the other system and $3a + 8b = 2$. Substituting a and b for x and y in the second equation gives $3a + 8b + k(2a - 5b) = 2 - 7k$. Using the two true equations above, substitute 2 for $3a + 8b$ and -7 for $2a - 5b$ gives $2 + k(-7) = 2 - 7k$, which is an identity and true for any value of k.

Problem 21

Solve the system $\begin{cases} x - 4y = 3 \\ 2x + y = -3 \end{cases}$

The first equation of the system is $x - 4y = 3$. This equation can easily be solved for x, resulting in the equation $x = 4y + 3$. Substitute this expression for x into the other equation and solve for y:

$2x + y = -3$

$2(4y + 3) + y = -3$

$8y + 6 + y = -3$

$9y = -9$

$y = -1$

Substitute -1 for y in the equation $2x + y = -3$ gives $2x = -2$, and

$x = -1$. The solution of the system is therefore $(-1, -1)$.

Problem 22

Use a graph to approximate the solution of the system $\begin{cases} -x + y = 9 \\ 2x + y = 5 \end{cases}$ to the nearest integer values of x and y.

The solution to a linear system is the intersection of the graphs of the system. The equations can be sketched by using the x- and y- intercepts of each line. For example, for $-x + y = 9$, the x- and y- intercepts are $(-9, 0)$ and $(0, 9)$, respectively. The intercepts for the other equation are determined similarly.

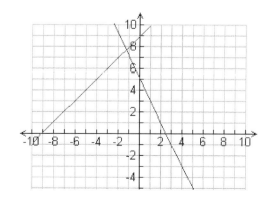

- 37 -

The intersection point is in the second quadrant. To the nearest integer values of x and y, the solution is $(-1, 8)$.

Problem 23

Solve the system $\begin{cases} \frac{x}{2} + \frac{y}{3} = -1 \\ \frac{x}{5} - \frac{y}{3} = 1 \end{cases}$. Describe your solution method.

To solve the system, multiply each equation by the least common denominator, or LCD. This will eliminate the fractions, and transform the system into one with integer coefficients.

$$\begin{cases} \left(\frac{x}{2} + \frac{y}{3} = -1\right) 6 \\ \left(\frac{x}{5} - \frac{y}{3} = 1\right) 15 \end{cases}$$

$$\begin{cases} 3x + 2y = -6 \\ 3x - 5y = 15 \end{cases}$$

Subtracting the equations results in the equation $7y = -21$, so $y = -3$. Substitute -3 for y into $3x + 2y = -6$ to get $3x = 0$, so $x = 0$. The solution of the system is $(0, -3)$.

Problem 24

At what point or points does the line $y = -x + 2$ intersect a circle with radius 2 and center at the origin?

The equation of a circle centered at the origin with radius r is $x^2 + y^2 = r^2$. For a radius of 2, this becomes $x^2 + y^2 = 4$. Substitute the expression $-x + 2$ for y in the equation of the circle, and solve for x:

$x^2 + y^2 = 4$

$x^2 + (-x + 2)^2 = 4$

$x^2 + x^2 - 4x + 4 = 4$

$2x^2 - 4x = 0$

$2x(x - 2) = 0$

$x = 0, x = 2$

If $x = 0$, then $y = -(0) + 2 = 2$. If $x = 2$, the $y = -(2) + 2 = 0$. The points of intersection, then, are $(0, 2)$ and $(2, 0)$.

Problem 25

Solve the system $\begin{cases} 3x - y = 6 \\ y = 4 - x^2 \end{cases}$, and find any intersection points.

The first equation of the system can be rewritten as $y = 3x - 6$. Substitute the expression $3x - 6$ for y in the quadratic equation:

$y = 4 - x^2$

$3x - 6 = 4 - x^2$

$x^2 + 3x - 10 = 0$

$(x + 5)(x - 2) = 0$

$x = -5, x = 2$

If $x = -5$, then $y = 3(-5) - 6 = -21$. If $x = 2$, then $y = 3(2) - 6 = 0$. The points of intersection are $(-5, -21)$ and $(2, 0)$.

Problem 26

Solve the system $\begin{cases} y = 4 - x^2 \\ y - 3 = 0 \end{cases}$ by graphing.

The equation $y = 4 - x^2$, which can be written as $y = -x^2 + 4$, represents a parabola that opens downward with vertex at $(0, 4)$. The equation $y - 3 = 0$ can be written as $y = 3$, the equation of a horizontal line passing through the point $(0, 3)$. The graph of the equations is shown below.

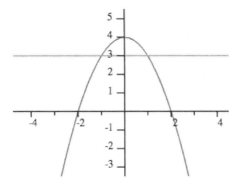

There are two points of intersection of the graphs, $(-1, 3)$ and

$(1, 3)$. These are the solutions to the system; both points check out algebraically.

Linear Equations and Inequalities

Function and relation

When expressing functional relationships, the variables x and y are typically used. These values are often written as the coordinates, (x,y). The x-value is the independent variable and the y-value is the dependent variable. A relation is a set of data in which there is not a unique y-value for each x-value in the data set. This means that there can be two of the same x-values assigned to different y-values. A relation is simply a relationship between the x and y-values in each coordinate but does not apply to the relationship between the values of x and y in the data set. A function is a relation where one quantity depends on the other. For example, the amount of money that you make depends on the number of hours that you work. In a function, each x-value in the data set has one unique y-value because the y-value depends on the x-value.

Determining if an equation or table represents a function

You can determine whether an equation is a function by substituting different values into the equation for x. These values are called input values. All possible input values are referred to as the domain. The result of substituting these values into the equation is called the output, or range. You can display and organize these numbers in a data table. A data table contains the values for x and y, which you can also list as coordinates. In order for a function to exist, the table cannot contain any repeating x-values that correspond with different y-values. If each x-coordinate has a unique y-coordinate, the table contains a function. However, there can be repeating y-values that correspond with different x-values. An example of this is when the function contains an exponent. For example, if $x^2 = y$, $2^2 = 4$, and $(-2)^2 = 4$.

Writing an equation using independent and dependent variables

To write an equation, you must first assign variables to the unknown values in the problem and then translate the words and phrases into expressions containing numbers and symbols. For example, if Ray earns $10 an hour, this can be represented by the expression $10x$, where x is equal to the number of hours that Ray works. The value of x represents the number of hours because it is the independent variable, or the amount that you can choose and can manipulate. To find out how much money, y, he earns in x hours, you would write the equation, $10x = y$. The variable y is the dependent variable because it depends on x and cannot be manipulated. Once you have the equation for the function, you can choose any number of hours to find the corresponding amount that he earns. For example, if you want to know how much he would earn working 36 hours, you would substitute 36 in for x and multiply to find that he would earn $360.

Graphing a function

To graph a function, first create a table of values based on the equation modeled in the problem. Choose x-values (at least 2 for linear functions, more for quadratic) for the table and then substitute them into the equation to find the corresponding y-values. Use each x and y value as a coordinate pair and plot these points on the coordinate grid. Next, connect the points with a line. The graph of a function will show a relationship among the coordinates in that there are no two y-values assigned to each x-value. The vertical line test is used to determine whether a graph contains a function. This states that if you pass a vertical line anywhere along the graph, it will only pass through the graph at one point. If it passes through the graph at more than one point, it is not considered a function.

Using a table to write a function rule

If given a set of data, place the corresponding x and y-values into a table and analyze the relationship between them. Consider what you can do to each x-value to obtain the corresponding y-value. Try adding or subtracting different numbers to and from x and then try multiplying or dividing different numbers to and from x. If none of these operations give you the y-value, try combining the operations. Once you find a rule that works for one pair, make sure to try it with each additional set of ordered pairs in the table. If the same operation or combination of operations satisfies each set of coordinates, then the table contains a function. The rule is then used to write the equation of the function in "$y =$" form.

Graphs of linear and quadratic functions

Linear functions are in the form, $y = x$ and when graphed form a straight line. To graph a function, you need to find at least two points on the line. Choose values for x and substitute them into the equation. Since $y = x$, then $0 = 0, 1 = 1, 2 = 2$, etc. This means that the coordinates $(0, 0), (1, 1)$, and $(2, 2)$ all lie on the line. Quadratic functions are in the form, $y = x^2$ and when graphed form a u-shaped parabola. Every x-value is squared, or multiplied by itself. After multiplying, you will find that the coordinates $(-2, 4), (1, 1)$, and $(2, 4)$ all lie on the parabola. The graphs extend infinitely in both directions and contain an infinite number of points. These graphs are called the parent functions of linear and quadratic equations because they are the most basic in their family of functions; the equations do not contain any coefficients or constants.

Domain, range, continuous data, and discrete data

The domain of a function is the set of all of the possible x-values. These are the values that make the function true. The domain is expressed using inequality symbols and brackets. Often, the domain is all real numbers since these numbers satisfy many functions. The range of a function is the set of all possible y-values, or the result of the values in the domain. To find the range, you substitute the domain values into the equation and express the result within a set of brackets. Linear and quadratic functions contain continuous data. This means the data is represented in an interval and represents a range of data values. This type of data is displayed on the graph with a smooth line and all points on the line are a part of the solution set. Since there are an infinite number of points on a line, we know this represents continuous data. Discrete data values are specific, distinct numbers. This data can be counted and is displayed on the graph as points, or coordinates. The data represented in a scatter plot is an example of discrete data.

Scatter plot

Scatter plots show the relationship between two sets of data. The first step in creating a scatter plot is to collect data. Suppose you are analyzing the relationship between age and hours of sleep. You would collect a representative sample of the population using a list or chart to organize your data. Next, you would arrange the data in a table with the independent variable on the left-hand side and the dependent variable on the right-hand side. To graph your data, look at the range in the values. In this situation, the independent variable, or x-values, and the dependent variable, or y-values, all are positive so you only need to draw and label Quadrant I on the coordinate grid. Look at the data and find the most appropriate intervals to label the axes. Plot the points using (x, y), moving over x

- 41 -

units on the horizontal axis and up y units on the vertical axis to see the relationship between the two data sets.

Correlation

A scatter plot is a way to represent the relationship between two data sets. The data can have one of three types of relationships, or correlations: a positive correlation, a negative correlation, or no correlation. A positive correlation is one in which the points increase from left to right. A negative correlation is one in which the points decrease from left to right. A scatter plot with no correlation is one in which the points show no relationship and neither rise nor fall. The correlation can help to determine the line of best fit. The line of best fit is a line drawn to best represent the data values. The line usually falls in the middle of the group of points and contains as many points as possible. When a graph has a positive or negative correlation, a line of regression can be drawn to determine an equation based on the relationship. When a graph has no correlation, a regression line cannot be drawn.

Simplifying polynomial expressions

Polynomials are a group of monomials added or subtracted together. Simplifying polynomials requires combining "like" terms. The "like" terms in a polynomial expression are those that have the same variable raised to the same power. It is often helpful to connect the "like" terms with arrows or lines in order to separate them from the other monomials. Once you have determined the "like" terms, you can re-arrange the polynomial by placing them together. Remember to include the sign that is in front of each term. Once the "like" terms are placed together, you can apply each operation and simplify. When adding and subtracting polynomials, only add and subtract the coefficient, or the number part; the variable and exponent stay the same.

Commutative, associative, and distributive properties

The commutative property states that changing the order of the terms in an equation will not change the outcome. You can remember this because "commute" means to move, or travel. For example, $5 + 4 = 9$ and moving the order of the terms, $4 + 5 = 9$, is also true. The commutative property is also true for multiplication: $5 \times 4 = 20$ and $4 \times 5 = 20$. The associative property states that when adding or multiplying, it doesn't matter how you group the terms, the result will be the same. Remember that simplifying within the parenthesis is the first step in using the order of operations. For example, $(2 + 3) + 4 = 9$ and $2 + (3 + 4) = 9$. This simplifies to $5 + 4 = 9$ and $2 + 7 = 9$. Using multiplication $2(3 \times 4) = 24$ and $(2 \times 3)4 = 24$. This simplifies to $2(12) = 24$ and $6(4) = 24$. You can remember this rule because the numbers are grouped, or "associated", with one another. The distributive property states that you multiply the number on the outside of the parenthesis by each number or value on the inside of the parenthesis. For example, $3(5 + 2) = 3(5) + 3(2)$. You can use arrows to help organize your work. Think of distributing as "giving something out."

Equation notation and function notation

Equations use numbers to show the equality of two expressions and use the variables x and y. Equation notation is written in "$y =$" form. Given an equation, you can find values for x and y by inputting a value for x and solving for y. These values are displayed as ordered pairs in a table of values. The ordered pairs can then be used as coordinates to graph the equation. An equation is a function if there is a unique relationship between x and y in that for every x-value, there is only one unique y-value. This can be determined from the graph using the vertical line test, in which a function exists if a vertical line can pass through the line at only one point. Function notation is

- 42 -

written in the "$f(x)$" form. The notation y and $f(x)$ are essentially the same, one just refers to an equation and one refers to a function. Knowing that an equation is a function can give you more information about its graph. Functions use equations to represent relationships between quantities. All functions have equations but not all equations are functions.

Domain and range of a function

The domain of a function is all of the possible x-values. The range of a function is all of the possible y-values. You can determine the domain and range of the function by visually inspecting the graph. First look at the domain, or x-values. Where do the x-values begin, and where do they end? This will establish the set of possible x-values. If the values extend indefinitely in both directions from zero, then the domain is all Real Numbers. Next, look at the range, or y-values, and determine the lowest and highest values for y. If the y-values extend indefinitely, then the range is all Real Numbers. Write your domain and range and include any restrictions.

Forms of linear equations

Linear equations can be written in three different forms, each used for a different purpose. The standard form of linear equations is $Ax + By = C$, where A, B and C are integers and A is a positive number. Any equation can be written in this form. This is helpful in solving and graphing systems of equations, where you must compare two or more equations. You can graph an equation in standard form by finding the intercepts. Determine the x-intercept by substituting zero in for y and vice versa. Next, the slope-intercept form of an equation is $y = mx + b$, where m is equal to the slope and b is equal to the y-intercept. You can graph an equation in this form by first plotting the y-intercept. If b is -2, you know that the y-intercept is equal to $(0, -2)$. From this point you can use the slope to create an additional point. If the slope is 4, or $\frac{4}{1}$, you would rise, or move up 4 units and run, or move over 1 unit from the y-intercept. Finally, the point-slope form of an equation is useful when you know the slope and a point on the line. It is written as $y - y_1 = m(x - x_1)$, where m is equal to the slope and (x_1, y_1) is a point on the line. You can graph an equation in point-slope form by plotting the given point and using the slope to plot additional points on the line.

Slope

The slope is the steepness or slant of a line. The steeper the line is, the larger the slope. It can be found on the graph by calculating the change in the y-values divided by the change in the x-values. The formula for slope is $m = \frac{(y_2 - y_1)}{(x_2 - x_1)}$, where (x_1, y_1) and (x_2, y_2) are any two points from the line. The slope of the line gives you an idea of how the data changes. If the line has a positive slope, you know that the data values steadily increase. If the line has a negative slope, the data values steadily decrease. A horizontal line indicates that there is a slope of 0. This is because the y-values do not change and 0 divided by anything is 0. A vertical line has no slope since the x-values do not change. You cannot divide a number by zero, so we say that this line has no slope. Understanding how to find the slope will allow you to write equations in slope-intercept and point-slope form.

Intercepts

The x-intercept is the point on the graph where the line crosses the x-axis. The y-value along the x-axis at this point is 0. The y-intercept is the point of the graph where the line crosses the y-axis. The x-value along the y-axis at this point is 0. This means that to find the x-intercept, you can substitute 0 in for y and to find the y-intercept, you can substitute 0 in for x into the equation. The standard form of an equation makes it easy to find the intercepts using this rule. Once you find the

x and y-intercepts, plot the two points and connect them to form a line. The x-intercepts of the graph are also called the roots of the function. The roots give you the number of solutions that an equation has. Since a linear function forms a line, it only crosses the x-axis at one point and therefore only has one solution.

Changing the slope and y-intercept

The slope is the steepness or slant of a line. If you change the value of the slope, it changes the steepness or slant of the line. A positive slope is one that increases from left to right. For example, a line with a slope of 5 increases very quickly, while a line with a slope of $\frac{2}{3}$ increases very slowly. A negative slope is one that decreases from left to right. For example, a line with a slope of $-\frac{1}{2}$ decreases slower than a line with a slope of -6. The y-intercept is the point that the line crosses the y-axis. Changing the y-intercept only raises or lowers the position of the line on the graph. A positive y-intercept falls above the origin and a negative y-intercept falls below the origin.

Direct and inverse variation

A direct variation is one in which the values for x are directly proportional to the values for y. This is expressed as a line on the graph that either steadily increases or decreases. The equation of a direct variation is written as $y = kx$, where k is called the constant of proportionality because y varies directly with x. An inverse variation is one in which the values for x are inversely proportional to the values for y. The graph of an inverse relationship is expressed as a line that curves inward toward the vertex and approaches the x and y-axes but never actually touches them. The equation of an inverse variation is written as $y = \frac{k}{x}$, because y varies inversely with x. A linear function can be a direct variation if the values are proportional. In this situation, the constant of proportionality is relative to the slope, or rate of change of a linear function.

Translating situations into linear inequalities

Inequalities compare two expressions that are not equal. One expression can be greater than, less than, greater than or equal to, or less than or equal to the other expression. Inequality symbols are used to express these comparisons. To translate a situation into an inequality, you must analyze the words that correspond with these symbols. The terms less than or fewer refer to the symbol <. The terms greater than or more refer to the symbol >. The terms less than or equal to, at most, or no more than, refer to the symbol ≤. Finally, the terms greater than or equal to, at least, and no less than, refer to the symbol ≥. When translating, choose a variable to represent the unknown value and then change the words or phrases into symbols. Recall the terms and expressions used to identify addition (sum, increased by, more, total), subtraction (difference, decreased by, less), multiplication (product, of, times, factor) and division (quotient, out of, ratio). For example, if the sum of 2 and a number is at most 12, then you would write, $2 + b \leq 12$.

Solving linear inequalities

Solving linear inequalities is very similar to solving linear equations. You must isolate the variable on one side of the inequality by using the inverse, or opposite operations. To undo addition, you use subtraction and vice versa. To undo multiplication, you use division and vice versa. The only difference in solving linear inequalities occurs when you multiply or divide by a negative number. When this is the case, you must flip the inequality symbol. This means that less than becomes greater than, greater than becomes less than, etc. Another type of inequality is called a compound inequality. A compound inequality contains two inequalities separated by an "and" or an "or"

- 44 -

statement. An "and" statement can also consist of a variable sandwiched in the middle of two inequality symbols. To solve this type of inequality, simply separate it into two inequalities applying the middle terms to each. Then, follow the steps to isolate the variable.

Systems of equations

A system of equations is a set of 2 or more equations with the same variables. You can solve systems using the substitution method, the elimination method, matrices, or by graphing the systems. The solution of a system of equations is the value that both or all of the equations share. When looking at the graph of a system, the solution is the point that is shared by all of the equations. These systems are considered consistent because there is always only one solution. Systems can also be inconsistent (when the lines are parallel and there is no solution) or dependent (when the lines are the same and there is infinitely many solutions). Systems are often used to compare situations that involve cost. For example, suppose you are trying to cut costs on your monthly cell phone bill. Company A charges $30 a month for a data plan plus an additional $0.10 per minute to talk and company B charges $50 a month for a data plan and an additional $0.05 per minute to talk. You can write an equation for each situation and then use systems to find out how many minutes you would have to talk for the cost to be the same. This will allow you to determine which cell plan is the better deal for the average number of minutes that you talk per month.

Solving systems of equations and solving systems of inequalities

Solving systems of inequalities is very similar to solving systems of equations in that you are looking for a solution or a range of solutions that satisfy all of the equations in the system. Since solutions to inequalities are within a certain interval, it is best to solve this type of system by graphing. Follow the same steps to graph an inequality as you would an equation, but in addition, shade the portion of the graph that represents the solution. Recall that when graphing an inequality on the coordinate plane, you replace the inequality symbol with an equal sign and draw a solid line if the points are included (greater than or equal to or less than or equal to) or a dashed line if the points are not included (greater than or less than). Then replace the inequality symbol and shade the portion of the graph that is included in the solution. Choose a point that is not on the line and test it in the inequality to see if it is makes sense. In a system, you repeat this process for all of the equations and the solution is the region in which the graphs overlap. This is unlike solving a system of equations, in which the solution is a single point where the lines intersect.

Quadratic function

A quadratic function is a function in the form $y = ax^2 + bx + c$, where a does not equal 0. While a linear function forms a line, a quadratic function forms a parabola, which is a u-shaped figure that either opens upward or downward. A parabola that opens upward is said to be a positive quadratic function and a parabola that opens downward is said to be a negative quadratic function. The shape of a parabola can differ, depending on the values of a, b, and c. All parabolas contain a vertex, which is the highest possible point, the maximum, or the lowest possible point, the minimum. This is the point where the graph begins moving in the opposite direction. A quadratic function can have zero, one, or two solutions, and therefore, zero, one, or two x-intercepts. Recall that the x-intercepts are referred to as the zeros, or roots, of a function. A quadratic function will have only one y-intercept. Understanding the basic components of a quadratic function can give you an idea of the shape of its graph.

- 45 -

Changing values in a quadratic equation change the position of a parabola

A quadratic function is written in the form $y = ax^2 + bx + c$. Changing the leading coefficient, a, in the equation changes the direction of the parabola. If the value of a is positive, the graph opens upward. The vertex of this parabola is the minimum value of the graph. If the value of a is negative, the graph opens downward. The vertex of this parabola is the maximum value of the graph. The leading coefficient, a, also affects the width of the parabola. The closer a is to 0, the wider the parabola will be. The values of b and c both affect the position of the parabola on the graph. The effect from changing b depends on the sign of a. If a is negative, increasing the value of b moves the parabola to the right and decreasing the value of b moves it to the left. If a is positive, changes to b have the opposite effect. The value of c in the quadratic equation represents the y-intercept and therefore, moves the parabola up and down the y-axis. The larger the c-value, the higher the parabola is on the graph.

Solving quadratic equations

One way to find the solution or solutions of a quadratic equation is to use its graph. The solution(s) of a quadratic equation are the values of x when $y = 0$. On the graph, $y = 0$ is where the parabola crosses the x-axis, or the x-intercepts. This is also referred to as the roots, or zeros of a function. Given a graph, you can locate the x-intercepts to find the solutions. If there are no x-intercepts, the function has no solution. If the parabola crosses the x-axis at one point, there is one solution and if it crosses at two points, there are two solutions. Since the solutions exist where $y = 0$, you can also solve the equation by substituting 0 in for y. Then, try factoring the equation by finding the factors of ac that add up to equal b. You can use the guess and check method, the box method, or grouping. Once you find a pair that works, write them as the product of two binomials and set them equal to zero. Finally, solve for x to find the solutions. The last way to solve a quadratic equation is to use the quadratic formula. The quadratic formula is $x = \frac{-b \pm \sqrt{b^2 - 4ac}}{2a}$. Substitute the values of a, b, and c into the formula and solve for x. Remember that $\pm$ refers to two different solutions. Always check your solutions with the original equation to make sure they are valid.

Exponential growth and decay functions

Exponential functions are written in the form $f(x) = Ab^x$, where A and b are positive and b is not equal to 1. Exponential functions have a domain of $0 \le x < \infty$. When b is greater than 1, the function represents exponential growth; when b is less than 1, it represents exponential decay. A can be thought of as the initial value of the function, since the function is equal to A when x equals 0. In exponential growth, the function's value begins at A and increases without bound, increasing by a factor of b every time x increases by 1. In exponential decay, the function's value begins at A and decreases to approach 0. The value decreases by a factor of b every time x increases by 1. Deposited money earning continuous interest is an example of growth that can be modeled exponentially, while the decay of radioactive isotopes is an example of exponential decay.

Example problems

Problem 1

Suppose that the distance Greg travels in his car is represented by the function, $y = x - 5$, where x is equal to the time that it takes him to get to his destination and y is equal to his total distance in miles. How many miles would Greg travel in 90 minutes? Explain how you can use this function to find information about future data.

If you know the equation of a function, you can determine any value for x and y. Since x is the independent variable, it is the value that you can manipulate. The dependent variable is y because you cannot manipulate, or change, the result. You can choose any value for x to find the corresponding y-value. For example, if it takes Greg 90 minutes to get to his grandmother's house, you can substitute 90 for x to find the total distance. $90 - 5 = 85$, so Greg traveled 85 miles. Using functions and understanding the relationship between distance and time, Greg can determine when he needs to leave for school, work, trips, etc. in order to effectively schedule himself and arrive at the appropriate time.

Problem 2

Consider the following situation: you drive 12 miles to school and maintain a constant speed until you hit traffic at 7:40 am. Once the traffic clears you resume your original speed until you get to school. Explain what the graph of this function would look like.

First, consider the variables that are involved in this situation. You are comparing the miles that you travel to school and the time that it takes you to get there. On the graph, the line that is formed by this relationship represents the speed that you travel. The graph should contain the correct labels and scales with the independent variable, the time, along the x-axis and the dependent variable, the distance, along the y-axis. If you maintain a constant speed, the graph would show a diagonal line increasing from zero. When you are stopped in traffic at 7:40 am, the distance is no longer increasing, however, the time is. Therefore, you would see the line continuing horizontally for a period of time. When the traffic clears, the line would again increase diagonally to represent the resumed speed. You can use the graph to analyze trends in the data in order to predict future events.

Problem 3

List the steps to find g(-3) if $g(x) = 2x^2 + x - 1$.

Substitute (-3) in for every value of x in the function:

$$g(-3) = 2(-3)^2 + (-3) - 1$$

Use the order of operations to simplify. First, simplify the exponents by squaring (-3):

$$g(-3) = 2(9) - 3 - 1$$

Multiply and divide from left to right:

$$g(-3) = 18 - 4$$

Add and subtract from left to right:

$$g(-3) = 14$$

Problem 4

Explain how to find the solution set of $x - 1 \leq -6$ given a replacement set of $\{-7, -2, 0, 6\}$.

- 47 -

To find the solution set, substitute each of the values in the replacement set in for x and determine whether the result satisfies the inequality. Remember that values less than or equal to -6 are all of the values to the left of -6 on the number line, including -6. Inputting -7 into the inequality results in $-8 \leq -6$. This is a true statement. Inputting -2 results in $-3 \leq -6$. This is a false statement. Inputting 0 results in $-1 \leq -6$, which is a false statement. Finally, inputting 6 results in $5 \leq -6$, which is also a false statement. Therefore, the only value from the replacement set that makes sense and satisfies the inequality is 7. The solution is written in set notation using brackets as $\{7\}$.

Problem 5

Describe how to write an equation given the coordinates: $(2,4), (3,5), (4,6), (5,7), and\ (6,8)$.

To write an equation given a function's coordinates, you must first place the ordered pairs into a table of values containing a column of x-values and a column of the corresponding y-values. Next, analyze the relationship between each x and y value and identify a pattern. Look at the first pair of numbers and determine what you can do to each x-value to get y-value as a result. The first pair is $(2,4)$, so you could either add two or multiply by two to get a result of four. Choose one of the operations and apply it to the other ordered pairs in the table. The next pair is $(3,5)$ and $3 + 2 = 5$, but $3 \times 2 \neq 5$. Once you find an operation that satisfies all of the pairs in the table, you can write an equation. Since adding by two is a consistent pattern, the equation that satisfies these coordinates is $y = x + 2$. Check your equation by substituting the remaining numbers from the table into the equation.

Problem 6

Explain the steps required in solving: $15 = -2x + 3$.

To solve an equation, first combine any "like" terms. "Like" terms are those that contain the same variables held to the same power or constants. Next, use inverse operations to isolate the variable on one side of the equation. Since both sides of an equation must remain equal, perform the same operation to both sides so that it remains balanced. When solving multi-step equations, first undo addition and subtraction followed by multiplication and division. In this equation, since the opposite of addition is subtraction, first subtract 3 from both sides of the equation. This simplifies to $12 = -2x$. Next, the opposite, or inverse, of multiplication is division so divide both sides by -2. This results in $-6 = x$, or $x = -6$. When solving equations, always verify your answer by substituting your solution back in to the original equation.

Problem 7

Explain how to determine the missing value in the following coordinates of a function: $(-2, -3), (-1, -2), (0, -1), (1, 0), (2, \_)$.

First, organize the coordinates into a table of values to display the relationships between x and y. A table represents a linear function if there is a consistent pattern between the x and y-values. You must be able to apply the same operation or combination of operations to each x-value to obtain the corresponding y-value. If there is a consistent pattern, a linear equation can be written. Looking at the

- 48 -

ordered pairs, you will see that you can subtract 1 from each x-value to obtain the corresponding y-value. Therefore, the equation can be written as, $y = x - 1$. Thus you can input the last x-value of 2 to find the corresponding y-value: $2 - 1 = 1$, so 1 is the missing value.

Problem 8

Describe the method used to find the slope of a line given the equation: $\frac{1}{2}y + 4 = x$.

Given an equation, you can find the slope by rewriting the equation in slope-intercept form. Slope-intercept form is $y = mx + b$, where m is equal to the slope and b is equal to the y-intercept. To rewrite the equation, use inverse operations to move the terms to the corresponding positions and determine the value of m. In the equation $\frac{1}{2}y + 4 = x$, to isolate y, you have to first undo any addition or subtraction. The opposite of addition is subtraction, so subtract 4 from both sides of the equation. This results in $\frac{1}{2}y = x - 4$. Next, y is multiplied by $\frac{1}{2}$ and to undo multiplication, divide both sides by $\frac{1}{2}$. Dividing by a fraction is the same as multiplying by its reciprocal, so multiply both sides by 2. Remember to use the distributive property to multiply 2 by the entire quantity $(x - 4)$. This results in, $y = 2x - 8$; therefore by the slope-intercept form, m or slope is equal to 2.

Problem 9

Describe two methods to find the x and y-intercepts of a line given the following table of values:

x	y
-2	-7
-1	-6
0	-5
1	-4
2	-3

The x-intercept is the point on the graph where y is equal to 0 and the y-intercept is the point on the graph where x is equal to 0. First, begin by looking at the x-values in the table. If you see an ordered pair where x is zero, then the corresponding y-value is the y-intercept. Since when $x = 0, y = -5$, the y-intercept is -5. There are no y-values that equal 0, so the next step is to write an equation. One method is to look for patterns among the ordered pairs. Looking at each x-value, you can see that subtracting 5 gives you the corresponding y-values, so $y = x - 5$. Substituting 0 in for y gives you $0 = x - 5$, which simplifies to $x = 5$. Therefore, the x-intercept is 5. You can also use the slope formula to calculate the change in y-values over the change in x-values. Here, $m = 1$, so you can then substitute this value and the y-intercept, $b = -5$, into the slope-intercept form of an equation, $y = mx + b$. Additionally, you could use the point-slope form using a point from the table and the slope to write the equation.

Problem 10

List the steps required to graph an equation given the points: $(-2, -4)$ and $(-1, 6)$.

Label the ordered pairs, (x_1, y_1) and (x_2, y_2).

Using the equation, $m = \frac{(y_2 - y_1)}{(x_2 - x_1)}$, substitute the ordered pairs into the formula and simplify:

$m = \frac{6 - (-4)}{-1 - (-2)}$

Use the rules for subtracting integers to simplify:

$m = \frac{6 + 4}{-1 + 2}$

Use the rules for adding integers to simplify:

$m = \frac{10}{1}$

Divide to solve:

$m = 10$

Plot the points $(-2, -4)$ and $(-1, 6)$ on the coordinate grid.

Use the slope of 10 to rise ten units and run one unit in order to plot additional points on the graph.

Connect the points with a straight line.

Problem 11

Explain how to graph and write the equation of a line in slope-intercept form given the slope of 3 containing the point $(-2, 1)$.

To write an equation in slope-intercept form, use the point-slope form,

$y - y_1 = m(x - x_1)$. Substitute the slope of 2 into the formula for m and the point $(-2, 1)$ in for (x_1, y_1). Simplify by combining "like" terms and using the opposite operations to isolate y on one side of the equation. This will give you the equation in slope-intercept form, which is $y = 3x + 7$. To graph an equation given the slope and a point on the line, first plot the point, $(-2, 1)$ along the x and y-axis. Then using the slope, rise three units run one unit to create a second point. Recall that any number is a fraction over 1. Next, use the b-value of 7 from the slope-intercept form to plot the y-intercept. Remember at the y-intercept, x is equal to zero so the y-intercept is $(0, 7)$. Connect these points with a straight line.

Problem 12

Explain how to find the zeros of the function $f(x) = -2x + 5$.

The zeros of a function, also called the roots of the function, are the points where the function is equal to zero. On the graph, the zeros of a function are located at the points where the line crosses the x-axis, or the x-intercepts. Recall that at the x-intercept, $f(x)$ is equal to 0, so to find the roots of a function, calculate the x-intercept by substituting 0 in for $f(x)$. In the function $f(x) = -2x + 5 = 0$, isolate the term containing x and solve. $2x = 5$, or $x = 2.5$, so the root of the function is 2.5. Since there is only one root, the line crosses the x-axis at only one point.

Problem 13

Explain how to find the y-intercept and zeros of $-3x + 2y = 6$.

> To find the y-intercept of an equation written in standard form, find the point where $x = 0$ by substituting 0 in for x, which gives: $0 + 2y = 6$. This is the same as $2y = 6$. Next, the opposite of multiplication is division, so divide by 2. This results in $y = 3$. To find the zeros of a function, you simply find the x-intercept. The x-intercept is the point where $y = 0$, so substitute 0 in for y which gives: $-3x + 0 = 6$. This is the same as $-3x = 6$. Again, using inverse operations, divide by -3 to isolate the variable. This results in $x = -2$. Therefore, the y-intercept of the function is $y = 3$ and the zero of the function is $x = -2$.

Problem 14

Describe the graph of $4x - 2y = 12$.

> To find the attributes of a graph, you need to find the domain, range, x and y-intercepts, and the slope. It is also important to determine the shape of the graph. Since the highest power of x is 1, this is a linear function and will form a straight line on the graph. The equation is written in standard form, so you can easily determine the x and y-intercepts by substituting 0 in for the opposite variable. Plugging 0 in for x gives you $y = -6$ and plugging 0 in for y gives you $x = 3$. Therefore, the y-intercept is -6 and the x-intercept, or zero of the function is 3. To find the slope of the line, you can rewrite the equation in slope-intercept form by solving for y. To solve for y, use inverse operations and subtract $4x$ from both sides and then divide by -2. The slope-intercept form of the equation is $y = 2x - 6$. Since $y = mx + b$, where m is equal to the slope, the slope of the line is 2. This means that from each point on the graph, you rise 2 units and then and run 1 unit. Since the slope is positive, the line increases from left to right. The domain and range for this line is all Real Numbers, as the line extends indefinitely in both directions and has a slope.

Problem 15

List the steps used to write the equation of a line in slope-intercept form given the points $(-2, 6)$ and $(2, -2)$.

Use the slope formula, $m = \frac{(y_2 - y_1)}{(x_2 - x_1)}$ to find the slope of the line.

Substitute the values into the formula:

$$m = \frac{-2 - 6}{2 - (-2)}$$

Simplify using the integer rules:

$$m = -\frac{8}{4}, m = -2$$

Use the slope and one point to write the equation in point-slope form:

$$y - y_1 = m(x - x_1)$$

Substitute the values into the formula:

$$y - 6 = -2(x - (-2))$$

Simplify using integer rules and the distributive property:

$$y - 6 = -2x - 4$$

Rewrite the equation in slope-intercept form, $y = mx + b$, by adding 6 to both sides:

$$y = -2x + 2$$

Problem 16

Explain how to graph $10 > -2x + 4$.

In order to graph the inequality $10 > -2x + 4$, you must first solve for x. The opposite of addition is subtraction, so subtract 4 from both sides. This results in, $6 > -2x$. Next, the opposite of multiplication is division, so divide both sides by -2. Don't forget to flip the inequality symbol since you are dividing by a negative number. This results in $-3 < x$. You can rewrite this as $x > -3$. To graph an inequality, you create a number line and put a circle around the value that is being compared to x. If you are graphing a greater than or less than inequality, as the one shown, the circle remains open. This represents all of the values excluding -3. If the inequality happens to be a greater than or equal to or less than or equal to, you draw a closed circle around the value. This would represent all of the values including the number. Finally, take a look at the values that the solution represents and shade the number line in the appropriate direction. You are graphing all of the values greater than -3 and since this is all of the numbers to the right of -3, shade this region on the number line.

- 52 -

Problem 17

Explain how to determine whether $(-2, 4)$ is a solution of the inequality $y \geq -2x + 3$.

> To determine whether a coordinate is a solution of an inequality, you can either use the inequality or its graph. Using $(-2, 4)$ as (x, y), substitute the values into the inequality to see if it makes a true statement. This results in $4 \geq -2(-2) + 3$. Using the integer rules, simplify the right side of the inequality by multiplying and then adding. The result is $4 \geq 7$, which is a false statement. Therefore, the coordinate is not a solution of the inequality. You can also use the graph of an inequality to see if a coordinate is a part of the solution. The graph of an inequality is shaded over the section of the coordinate grid that is included in the solution. The graph of $y \geq -2x + 3$ includes the solid line $y = -2x + 3$ and is shaded to the right of the line, representing all of the points greater than and including the points on the line. This excludes the point $(-2, 4)$, so it is not a solution of the inequality.

Problem 18

List and define Describe how to solve the systems $x + y = 8$ and $-3x - y = 6$ using the substitution method.

> Solving systems using the substitution method involves solving one equation for a given variable and then substituting that value into the other equation. It does not matter which equation you choose to work with or which variable you isolate, the answer will be the same either way. Using mental math, you may notice that isolating a variable in the first equation requires only one step. If you choose to isolate the y, you would use the inverse operations and subtract x from both sides. This would result in $y = -x + 8$. Now, since you have solved one of the equations for y, you can substitute this value in for y in the other equation; $-3x - (-x + 8) = 6$. To solve for x, simplify using the integer rules. This results in, $-3x + x - 8 = 6$, or $-2x - 8 = 6$. Next, add 8 on both sides and the result is $-2x = 14$. Finally divide by -2 to see that $x = -7$. Remember that the solution to a system of equations is the value of both variables that make sense in all equations. Therefore, you must substitute -7 back into one of the equations to find the value for y: $-3(-7) - y = 6$ simplifies to $y = 15$, so the solution is $(-7, 15)$. Always substitute you answer back into both equations to verify that it is correct.

Problem 19

Explain how to solve the system $x + y = 5$ and $-2x + 2y = 14$ using the elimination method.

The elimination method involves adding or subtracting two linear equations that are written in the same form in order to eliminate, or remove, one of the variables. First, make sure that the equations are in the same form. Here, both equations are written in standard form. Next, look at the two x-values and the two y-values. Adding these values together would not eliminate either variable, so think of a number that you could multiply on one equation that would result in the one variable cancelling the other if the equations are added together. Multiplying the first equation by 2 would result in $2x + 2y = 10$, and since $2x + (-2x)$ 0, the x-variable would be eliminated when adding the equations. Choose a method and multiply the entire equation by that value. Line the equations up vertically and add them together. The sum of the x-values is 0, so you are left with, $4y = 24$. Using the inverse operations to isolate the variable, the result is $y = 6$. Finally, use this y-value and substitute it back into one of the original equations to find the value of x. $x + (6) = 5$ simplifies to $x = -1$, so the solution is $(-1, 6)$. Remember to plug these values back into both equations to verify that your answer is correct.

Problem 20

Compare the shape of the graph of $y = -2x^2$ to its parent function.

The parent function is the most basic function in each category. The parent function of a linear function is $y = x$. Recall that a quadratic function is in the form, $y = ax^2 + bx + c$. The parent function of a quadratic function is $y = x^2$. The graph of the quadratic parent function opens upward and is therefore, a positive function. The vertex of the function is at $(0, 0)$, the x-intercept is at $(0, 0)$, and the y-intercept of the function is also at $(0, 0)$. Unlike its parent function, the graph of $y = -2x^2$ opens downward and is a negative function (due to the negative coefficient on the x.) The width of each graph is also slightly different. The graph of $y = -2x^2$ is thinner than its parent function (due to the coefficient on the x being greater than 1.) However, like its parent function, this function also has a vertex of $(0, 0)$, as well as an x and y-intercept of $(0, 0)$. Understanding the components of a function compared to its parent function can help you to predict how changing the values of a, b, and c will affect the shape of its graph.

Problem 21

Describe how to find the roots of $y = x^2 + 6x - 16$ and explain why these values are important.

> The roots of a quadratic equation are the solutions when $ax^2 + bx + c = 0$. To find the roots of a quadratic equation, first replace y with 0. If $0 = x^2 + 6x - 16$, then to find the values of x, you can factor the equation if possible. When factoring a quadratic equation where $a = 1$, find the factors of c that add up to b. That is the factors of -16 that add up to 6. The factors of -16 include, -4 and 4, -8 and 2 and -2 and 8. The factors that add up to equal 6 are -2 and 8. Write these factors as the product of two binomials, $0 = (x - 2)(x + 8)$. You can verify that these are the correct factors by using FOIL to multiply them together. Finally, since these binomials multiply together to equal zero, set them each equal to zero and solve for x. This results in $x - 2 = 0$, which simplifies to $x = 2$ and $x + 8 = 0$, which simplifies to $x = -8$. Therefore, the roots of the equation are 2 and -8. These values are important because they tell you where the graph of the equation crosses the x-axis. The points of intersection are $(2, 0)$ and $(-8, 0)$.

Problem 22

List the steps used in solving $y = 2x^2 + 8x + 4$.

> First, substitute 0 in for y in the quadratic equation:

$$0 = 2x^2 + 8x + 4$$

> Next, factor the quadratic equation. If $a \neq 1$, list the factors of ac, or 8:

$$(1, 8), (-1, -8), (2, 4), (-2, -4)$$

> Look for the factors of ac that add up to b, or 8:

> Since the equation cannot be factored, substitute the values of a, b, and c into the quadratic formula, $x = \frac{-b \pm \sqrt{b^2 - 4ac}}{2a}$:

$$x = \frac{-8 \pm \sqrt{8^2 - 4(2)(4)}}{2(2)}$$

> Use the order of operations to simplify:

$$x = \frac{-8 \pm \sqrt{32}}{4}$$

> Reduce and simplify:

$$x = \frac{-8 \pm 4\sqrt{2}}{4}$$

$$x = 2 \pm \sqrt{2}$$

$$x = 2 + \sqrt{2} \text{ and } x = 2 - \sqrt{2}$$

- 55 -

Check both solutions with the original equation to make sure they are valid.

Simplify the square roots and round to two decimal places.

$$x = 3.41 \text{ and } x = 0.59$$

Problem 23

Explain how to multiply $(2x^4)^2(xy)^4 \cdot 4y^3$ using the laws of exponents.

According the order of operations, the first step in simplifying expressions to is to evaluate within the parenthesis. Moving from left to right, the first set of parenthesis contains a power raised to a power. The rules of exponents state that when a power is raised to a power, you multiply the exponents. Since $4 \times 2 = 8$, $(2x^4)^2$ can be written as $4x^8$. The second set of parenthesis raises a product to a power. The rules of exponents state that you raise every value within the parenthesis to the given power. Therefore, $(xy)^4$ can be written as x^4y^4. Combining these terms with the last term gives you, $4x^8 \cdot x^4y^4 \cdot 4y^3$. In this expression, there are powers with the same base. The rules of exponents state that you add powers with the same base, while multiplying the coefficients. You can group the expression as $(4x^8 \cdot x^4) \cdot (y^4 \cdot 4y^3)$ to organize the values with the same base. Then, using this rule add the exponents. The result is $4x^{12} \cdot 4y^7$, or $16y^{12}y^7$.

Problem 24

Describe how to find the value of y when $x = 8$ if y varies inversely with x and when $y = 24, x = 4$.

An inverse variation is a special relationship between two variables in which as one value increases, the other decreases. This relationship is represented by the equation $y = \frac{k}{x}$, where k is the constant of proportionality. The constant of proportionality is a way to express how the variables change. The first step in finding the missing value in the given relationship is to find the value of k. Use the formula and fill in the missing values. $24 = \frac{k}{4}$. Using inverse operations, you know that the opposite of division is multiplication, so multiply 4 on both sides. The result is $k = 96$. Now, using the formula again, you can find the missing value of y if $x = 8$ by substituting the values into the corresponding positions. The result is $y = \frac{96}{8}$, or $y = 12$. Therefore, if y varies inversely with x, then when $x = 8, y = 12$. You can check your result by looking at the relationship between the two x-values and the two y-values. Since they are inversely related, as the x-values double, the y-values are cut in half.

Polynomials and Rational Expressions and Equations

Polynomials are closed under multiplication

For a set to have closure under a particular operation, applying the operation to two elements of the set must result in a member of the set. This means that the product of any two polynomials results in another polynomial. This is correct, because every term of a polynomial in x is of the form ax^n, where a is a real number and n is a nonnegative integer. The product of any two such terms would be $ax^m \cdot bx^n = abx^{m+n}$, where ab is a real number and $m + n$ is a nonnegative integer. The last statement relies on the fact that real numbers are closed under multiplication, and nonnegative integers are closed under addition.

Example problems

Problem 1

Subtract the polynomial $3x^2 - 4x + 1$ from the polynomial $-2x^2 - x + 5$.

> To subtract polynomials, subtract like terms. Like terms have the same variable part, such as $3x^2$ and $-2x^2$, which are both are x^2 terms. To find the difference of like terms, find the difference of the coefficients, and retain the same variable part. You can use the distributive property to first distribute the subtraction to each term of the polynomial that is being subtracted.

$$(-2x^2 - x + 5) - (3x^2 - 4x + 1) =$$

$$(-2x^2 - x + 5) - 3x^2 + 4x - 1 =$$

$$(-2x^2 - 3x^2) + (-x + 4x) + (5 - 1) =$$

$$-5x^2 + 3x + 4$$

Problem 2

When a polynomial $P(x)$ is divided by $(x + 2)$, the remainder is -4. What is the value of

$P(-2)$?

> To solve this question, apply the Remainder Theorem for polynomials. The Remainder Theorem states that for a polynomial $P(x)$ and a real number a, the remainder when $P(x)$ is divided by
>
> $(x - a)$ is $P(a)$. Since $P(x)$ was divided by the factor $(x + 2)$, let $a = -2$ in the theorem. This means that $P(a) = P(-2)$, and this is equal to the remainder. Since the remainder is -4, it must be that
>
> $P(-2) = -4$. Note that it is not required to explicitly know the polynomial $P(x)$ or even its degree to apply the remainder theorem.

Problem 3

Divide the polynomial $x^2 + 2x - 4$ by $(x - 3)$. Verify the Remainder Theorem by evaluating the polynomial at $x = 3$.

Divide the polynomial $x^2 + 2x - 4$ by $(x - 3)$ using synthetic or long division:

$$
\begin{array}{r|rrr}
3 & 1 & 2 & -4 \\
  &   & 3 & 15 \\
\hline
  & 1 & 5 & 11
\end{array}
$$

$$
\begin{array}{r}
x \;\; + 5 \\
x - 3\,\overline{)\,x^2 + 2x - 4} \\
-x^2 + 3x \\
\hline
5x - 4 \\
-5x + 15 \\
\hline
R\ 11
\end{array}
$$

In either case, the remainder is 11. By the Remainder Theorem, for a polynomial $P(x)$ and a real number a, the remainder when $P(x)$ is divided by $(x - a)$ is $P(a)$. In this case, this means the remainder when $x^2 + 2x - 4$ is divided by $(x - 3)$ must be $P(3)$. Verify that $P(3) = 11$ by substituting $x = 3$ into the polynomial:

$(3)^2 + 2(3) - 4 = 9 + 6 - 4 = 11$

Problem 4

Let $P(x)$ be a cubic polynomial function such that $P(2) = P(-1) = P(4) = 0$. If the y-intercept of $P(x)$ is 2, what is the equation for $P(x)$?

By the Remainder Theorem, for a polynomial $P(x)$ and a real number a, the remainder when $P(x)$ is divided by $(x - a)$ is $P(a)$. This means that, since their remainders when divided into $P(x)$ are all zero,

$(x - 2)$, $(x + 1)$, and $(x - 4)$ are factors of $P(x)$. Because $P(x)$ is a cubic polynomial function, it must then be of the form $P(x) = a(x - 2)(x + 1)(x - 4)$, where a is some real number. To determine a, use the fact that the y-intercept is 2, which means that $P(0) = 2$:

$P(x) = a(x - 2)(x + 1)(x - 4)$

$P(0) = 2 = a(0 - 2)(0 + 1)(0 - 4) = 8a$

$2 = 8a$

$a = \frac{1}{4}$

The equation for $P(x)$, then, is $P(x) = \frac{1}{4}(x - 2)(x + 1)(x - 4)$.

Problem 5

Find the zeros of $y = 2x^2 + 3x - 5$ by factoring.

The zeros of $y = 2x^2 + 3x - 5$ are the values of x for which $y = 0$. These are also the x-intercepts of the graph of the function. Factor $2x^2 + 3x - 5$ and rewrite the equation as $y = (2x + 5)(x - 1)$. In factored form, the zeros are found by setting each linear factor equal to zero:

$$2x + 5 = 0 \qquad x - 1 = 0$$
$$2x = -5 \qquad\quad x = 1$$
$$x = -\frac{5}{2}$$

The zeros of $y = 2x^2 + 3x - 5$ are $x = 1$ and $x = \frac{5}{2}$.

Problem 6

Construct a rough graph of $y = x^3 - x^2 - 12x$.

To construct a rough graph of the function, factor the polynomial $x^3 - x^2 - 12x$ to find the zeros of $y = x^3 - x^2 - 12x$. Because $x^3 - x^2 - 12x = x(x^2 - x - 12) = x(x - 4)(x + 3)$, the function has zeros at $x = 0$, $x = 4$, and $x = -3$. The zeroes are x-intercepts of the graph of the function. The coefficient of the leading term x^3 is positive, and x^3 has an odd degree. Therefore the value of y will approach negative infinity as x goes to negative infinity, and approach positive infinity as x goes to positive infinity. Therefore, the value of y increases from $-\infty$ in the range $x = -\infty$ to $x = -3$ where $y = 0$, continues increasing to a local maximum before decreasing through $y = 0$ at $x = 0$ to some local minimum, and finally increases through $y = 0$ at $x = 4$ to $+\infty$ as x goes to $+\infty$. A rough sketch is shown.

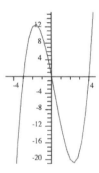

Problem 7

Sketch a cubic function with zeros at $x = -1$ and $x = 3$ that does not pass through the 4th quadrant. Explain your reasoning.

The cubic function has zeros at $x = -1$ and $x = 3$, so these will be x-intercepts of the function. The function does not pass through the 4th quadrant, which must mean that the curve is tangent to the x-axis at $(3, 0)$, and does not pass through the x-axis at this point. For this same reason, the value of y will approach negative infinity as x

- 59 -

goes to negative infinity, and approach positive infinity as x goes to positive infinity. A possible sketch is shown.

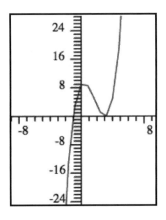

Problem 8

Write the equation for the parabola shown.

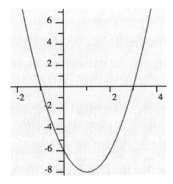

To determine the equation for the parabola, identify the zeros from the graph. The zeros are $x = -1$ and $x = 3$, which means that $(x + 1)$ and $(x - 3)$ are factors of the polynomial that represents the function. Since the parabola is the graph of a quadratic equation, write $y = a(x + 1)(x - 3)$. To determine the value of a, use the fact that the graph passes through the point $(0, -6)$:

$y = a(x + 1)(x - 3)$

$-6 = a(0 + 1)(0 - 3)$

$-6 = -3a$

$a = 2$

Therefore, the equation for the parabola is $y = 2(x + 1)(x - 3)$.

Problem 9

Tony has 4 sections of fence that are *m* feet long, and 4 sections of fence that are *n* feet long. He encloses two square areas with the fencing, one of side *m* and one of side *n*. How much more area can he enclose by making one large square area instead?

- 60 -

Sketch a diagram of what Tony did:

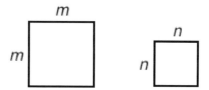

The total area of the enclosures is $m^2 + n^2$. Now sketch a diagram of how Tony could make one large enclosure:

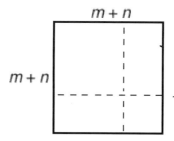

The total area of this enclosure is $(m + n)^2 = m^2 + 2mn + n^2$. Therefore one large fenced area encloses $2mn$ more square feet.

Problem 10

Explain how the expressions m, $\frac{m^2-1}{2}$, and $\frac{m^2+1}{2}$ can be used to generate Pythagorean triples for certain values of m.

A Pythagorean triple is a set of three positive integers that satisfy the Pythagorean Theorem, $a^2 + b^2 = c^2$. For example, the set of numbers {3, 4, 5} is a Pythagorean triple since $3^2 + 4^2 = 5^2$. To show how the given expressions can be used, show that the sum of the squares of two of the expressions equals the square of the remaining term:

$$m^2 + \left(\frac{m^2 - 1}{2}\right)^2 = m^2 + \left(\frac{m^2 - 1}{2}\right)\left(\frac{m^2 - 1}{2}\right) = m^2 + \frac{1}{4}(m^4 - 2m^2 + 1)$$

$$= \frac{1}{4}(4m^2 + m^4 - 2m^2 + 1) = \frac{1}{4}(m^4 + 2m^2 + 1)$$

$$= \frac{1}{4}(m^2 + 1)^2 = \left(\frac{m^2 + 1}{2}\right)^2$$

Clearly, the divisions by 2 require the numerators of those expressions to be even (in order to produce integer results). This occurs for odd m. For $m = 1$, though, one of the terms becomes 0, which is, of course, not allowable. Since negative m produce identical values, for odd m such that $|m| \geq 3$, the expressions generate Pythagorean triples

- 61 -

Problem 11

Show that the sum of the squares of three consecutive integers a, b, and c, is given by the expression $3b^2 + 2$, where b is the middle integer.

> Examples of three consecutive integers are 4, 5, and 6, or 21, 22, and 23. If x represents the middle of 3 consecutive integers, then the other two integers are given by the expressions $x + 1$ and $x - 1$. The squares of these expressions are x^2, $(x + 1)^2$, and $(x - 1)^2$. Now show that $x^2 + (x + 1)^2 + (x - 1)^2 = 3x^2 + 2$:
>
> $$x^2 + (x + 1)^2 + (x - 1)^2 =$$
>
> $$x^2 + x^2 + 2x + 1 + x^2 - 2x + 1 =$$
>
> $$3x^2 + 2$$

Problem 12

Expand the expression $(b - 2)^4$ using the Binomial Theorem.

> The Binomial Theorem is shown below.
>
> $(x + y)^n = a_0 x^n y^0 + a_1 x^{n-1} y^1 + a_2 x^{n-2} y^2 + \cdots + a_{n-1} x^1 y^{n-1} + a_n x^0 y^n$, where the coefficients $a_0, a_1, \ldots, a_n$ are given by the $(n + 1)$th row of Pascal's Triangle. Applying the formula with $x = b$ and $y = -2$ gives: $(b - 2)^4 = a_0 b^4 (-2)^0 + a_1 b^3 (-2)^1 + a_2 b^2 (-2)^2 + a_3 b^1 (-2)^3 + a_4 b^0 (-2)^4 = a_0 b^4 - 2a_1 b^3 + 4a_2 b^2 - 8a_3 b + 16a_4$
>
> The coefficients $a_0, a_1, \ldots, a_n$ are given by the 5th row of Pascal's Triangle, which is 1, 4, 6, 4, 1. So the expansion becomes
>
> $b^4 - 8b^3 + 24b^2 - 32b + 16$.

Problem 13

Write the 6th row of Pascal's Triangle. Describe what you did.

> Pascal's Triangle is a pattern of numbers that give the coefficients of the terms in a binomial expansion. The numbers in row $(n + 1)$ of the triangle represent the coefficients for the terms of the expansion $(x + y)^n$. The first 4 rows of the triangle are shown below:
>
> $$1$$
> $$1 \quad 1$$
> $$1 \quad 2 \quad 1$$
> $$1 \quad 3 \quad 3 \quad 1$$
>
> The pattern continues indefinitely, where each entry is the sum of the two entries diagonally above it. The first and last entries of every row are 1. Therefore, the next row of the triangle will be 1, 4, 6, 4, 1. The 6th row of Pascal's Triangle is 1, (1 + 4), (4 + 6), (6 + 4), (4 + 1), 1 = 1, 5, 10, 10, 5, 1.

Problem 14

What is the coefficient of the x^5 term in the expansion of $(2x - 1)^5$?

The Binomial Theorem gives the expansion of the expression

$(x + y)^n$, where x and y are real numbers and n is a positive integer. The theorem can be written as follows:

$(x + y)^n = a_0 x^n y^0 + a_1 x^{n-1} y^1 + a_2 x^{n-2} y^2 + \cdots + a_{n-1} x^1 y^{n-1} + a_n x^0 y^n$, where the coefficients $a_0, a_1, ..., a_n$ are given by the $(n + 1)$th row of Pascal's Triangle. Since n = 5, use the 6th row of the Triangle, which has the values 1, 5, 10, 10, 5, and 1. The x^5 term is the first term; $a_0 = 1$. The x^5 term is therefore $1(2x)^5(-1)^0 = 32x^5$. The coefficient of the x^5 term is 32.

Problem 15

Find the remainder when $2b^2 + 3b + 2$ is divided by $2b + 1$.

The remainder when $2b^2 + 3b + 2$ is divided by $2b + 1$ can be found by long division. To divide polynomials using long division, find the first term of the quotient by dividing $2b^2$ by $2b$, which gives b. Multiply this by the divisor to get $2b^2 + b$, and then subtract this result from the first two terms of the dividend to obtain $2b$. Then bring down the +2 to form $2b + 2$, and continue in this way. The complete division is shown below.

When the degree of the result after a subtraction is less than that of the divisor, the result is the remainder. So, the remainder is 1, and $2b^2 + 3b + 2$ divided by $2b + 1$ is equal to $b + 1 + \dfrac{1}{2b+1}$.

(Note: synthetic division cannot be used in this case, since the divisor is not a linear factor.)

Problem 16

Rewrite the rational expression $\dfrac{3x^3 + 2x^2}{x}$ by inspection.

The rational expression has a monomial for a denominator. This means that when each term of the numerator is divided by the denominator, the result of each division can be found by applying properties of exponents. In particular, the property $\dfrac{x^n}{x^m} = x^{n-m}$ can be used to rewrite each term as shown:

$$\frac{3x^3 + 2x^2}{x} = \frac{3x^3}{x} + \frac{2x^2}{x} = 3x^2 + 2x$$

The polynomial $3x^2 + 2x$ is equivalent to the original rational expression. Note that the only exception is the value $x = 0$, because the original rational expression is undefined for $x = 0$.

Problem 17

A computer program divides the polynomial $4b^5 + 3b^4 - 7b^2 + 3b - 2$ by the binomial

- 63 -

$3b - 2$. The output below shows the coefficients of the terms of the quotient, with the last value equal to the numerator of the remainder.

OUTPUT: 4 7 7 0   3 1

Write the rational expression that represents this result.

The polynomial that represents the dividend is of degree 5, and the divisor is a binomial of degree 1. This means that the first term of the quotient with be a term of degree 4. The numbers 4, 7, 7, 0, and 3 are therefore the coefficients of the terms with variable parts b^4, b^3, b^2, b, and then a constant term of 3. The 0 indicates that there is no b term. The denominator of the remainder is equal to the divisor $3b - 2$. The rational expression that equals $4b^5 + 3b^4 - 7b^2 + 3b - 2$ divided by the binomial $3b - 2$ is $4b^4 + 7b^3 + 7b^2 + 3 + \frac{1}{3b-2}$.

Problem 18

Add the expressions $\frac{1}{x+1} + \frac{x}{x+1}$ and simplify the result.

To add rational expressions, first obtain a common denominator. Then add the numerators, and keep the same denominator. Since the denominator of each expression is $x + 1$, the expressions can be added directly:

$$\frac{1}{x+1} + \frac{x}{x+1} = \frac{1+x}{x+1}$$

The expressions $1 + x$ and $x + 1$ are equivalent. By dividing the numerator and denominator by $x + 1$, the expression can be further simplified:

$$\frac{1+x}{x+1} = \frac{x+1}{x+1} = 1$$

The sum of the rational expressions is equal to 1. This is true for all values of x except $x = -1$, since the original expressions are undefined for $x = -1$.

Problem 19

What is the least common denominator of $\frac{3x}{x^2-x-6}$ and $\frac{2x}{x^2-6x+9}$?

To determine the least common denominator, or LCD, of two rational expressions, factor the denominators completely. The LCD is equal to the product of the greatest occurring power of each unique factor.

$x^2 - x - 6 = (x - 3)(x + 2)$

$x^2 - 6x + 9 = (x - 3)^2$

The unique factors are $(x + 2)$ and $(x - 3)$. The greatest occurring power of $(x - 3)$ is 2. Therefore the LCD of the two expressions is

$(x + 2)(x - 3)^2$.

Problem 20

Multiply the expressions $\frac{1-x}{x^2+2x+1}$ and $\frac{5}{x^2-1}$. Simplify the result.

To multiply two rational expressions, multiply the numerators to obtain the new numerator, and multiply the denominators to obtain the new denominator:

$$\frac{1-x}{x^2+2x+1} \cdot \frac{5}{x^2-1} = \frac{5(1-x)}{(x^2+2x+1)(x^2-1)}$$

To simplify the result, factor the numerator and denominator completely. The factor $1 - x$ in the numerator can be rewritten as

$-(x - 1)$, and the common factor $(x - 1)$ in the numerator and denominator can be cancelled:

$$\frac{5(1-x)}{(x^2+2x+1)(x^2-1)} = \frac{-5(x-1)}{(x+1)(x+1)(x+1)(x-1)} = \frac{-5}{(x+1)^3}$$

Note that this expression is equivalent to the original product for all x except $x = \pm 1$, since the original expressions are undefined for these values.

Problem 21

If $p(x)$ is a polynomial and $\frac{p(x)}{x-3}$ leaves a reminder of -6, what is $p(3)$?

By the Remainder Theorem, for a polynomial $p(x)$ and a real number a, the remainder when $p(x)$ is divided by $(x - a)$ is $p(a)$. In the given equation, $p(x)$ is divided by the binomial $x - 3$, and leaves a reminder of -6. This means that the value of $p(3)$ is -6. Note that the theorem can be applied without needing to know the actual terms of the polynomial $p(x)$.

Problem 22

What are the zeros of the polynomial $(2x - 1)(x^2 - 9)$?

The zeros of the polynomial can be determined by factoring. The expression

$x^2 - 9$ is a difference of squares, and factors as $(x - 3)(x + 3)$. The factored form of the full polynomial is therefore $(2x - 1)(x - 3)(x + 3)$. Set each of the linear factors equal to zero and solve for x:

$2x - 1 = 0$	$x - 3 = 0$
$x + 3 = 0$	$x = 3$
$2x = 1$	$x = -3$
$x = \frac{1}{2}$	

The zeros of the polynomial are $\frac{1}{2}$, 3, and –3.

Problem 23

Prove that the product of two consecutive even or odd integers is equal to 1 less than the square of their mean.

Let n represent the first of two consecutive even or odd integers. Then the following consecutive integer is given by the expression $n + 2$. The mean of the two numbers is $n + 1$, since $\frac{n+n+2}{2} = \frac{2n+2}{2} = n + 1$. One less than the square of this expression is written as $(n + 1)^2 – 1$. Show that this expression is equal to the product of the two consecutive even or odd integers by factoring the expression as a difference of squares:

$(n + 1)^2 – 1 = (n + 1 – 1)(n + 1 + 1) = (n + 0)(n + 2) = n(n + 2)$

Problem 24

What is the constant term in the expansion of $(-2 – 4m)^5$?

The Binomial Theorem gives the expansion of the expression

$(x + y)^n$, where x and y are real numbers and n is a positive integer. The theorem can be written as follows:

$(x + y)^n = a_0 x^n y^0 + a_1 x^{n-1} y^1 + a_2 x^{n-2} y^2 + \cdots + a_{n-1} x^1 y^{n-1} + a_n x^0 y^n$, where the coefficients $a_0, a_1, ..., a_n$ are given by the $(n + 1)$th row of Pascal's Triangle. For the expression $(-2 – 4m)^5$, let $x = -2$ and $y = 4m$ in the equation above. The first term, $a_0 x^n y^0$, must represent the constant term in this case, since the variable y is raised to the power of zero. Also, the first term in each row of Pascal's Triangle is one, so a_0 is 1. The constant term is therefore $1(-2)^5 = -32$.

Problem 25

Simplify the rational expression $\frac{x-1}{1-x^2}$.

To simplify a rational expression, factor the numerator and denominator completely. Factors that are the same and appear in the numerator and denominator have a ratio of 1. The denominator, $1 – x^2$, is a difference of squares. It can be factored as $(1 – x)(1 + x)$. The factor $1 – x$ and the numerator $x – 1$ are opposites, and have a ratio of –1. Rewrite the numerator as –1(1 – x). So, the rational expression can be simplified as follows:

$$\frac{x-1}{1-x^2} = \frac{-1(1-x)}{(1-x)(1+x)} = \frac{-1}{1+x}$$

(Note that since the original expression is defined for $x \neq \{-1, 1\}$, the simplified expression has the same restrictions.)

Problem 26

Alison knows that rational expressions are closed under division, assuming a nonzero divisor. She then claims that since all polynomials are rational expressions, polynomials are also closed under division, assuming a nonzero divisor. Explain her error.

Alison is correct that rational expressions are closed under division, assuming a nonzero divisor. She is also correct in saying that all polynomials are rational expressions, since the polynomial could be written with a denominator of 1, such as $3x^2 + 4 = \frac{3x^2+4}{1}$. However, closure of rational expressions only guarantees that dividing one rational expression by another results in a rational expression. Polynomials are a subset of the rational expressions, but the ratio of two polynomials is only a polynomial if the divisor is a nonzero constant. Since there are divisors of polynomials that do not yield polynomial quotients, polynomials are not closed under division.

Problem 27

Simplify the quotient: $\frac{x-2}{3x} \div \frac{x^2-4}{6x^2}$.

To simplify the quotient, first rewrite it as a product by taking the reciprocal of the divisor. Then completely factor the numerators and denominators, and simplify by recognizing identical factors in the numerator and the denominator have a ratio of 1:

$$\frac{x-2}{3x} \div \frac{x^2-4}{6x^2} =$$

$$\frac{x-2}{3x} \cdot \frac{6x^2}{x^2-4} =$$

$$\frac{x-2}{3x} \cdot \frac{2x(3x)}{(x-2)(x+2)} =$$

$$\frac{2x}{x+2}$$

- 67 -

Rational expressions are closed under subtraction using closure properties of polynomials

Rational expressions are closed under subtraction if the difference of any two rational expressions results in a rational expression. Consider two rational expressions $\frac{a(x)}{b(x)}$ and $\frac{c(x)}{d(x)}$, where $a(x)$, $b(x)$, $c(x)$, and $d(x)$ are polynomials. Their difference can be written as follows:

$$\frac{a(x)}{b(x)} - \frac{c(x)}{d(x)} = \frac{a(x) \cdot d(x) - b(x) \cdot c(x)}{b(x) \cdot d(x)}$$

Since polynomials are closed under multiplication, the products in the right side of the equation (including the denominator) are all polynomials. Since polynomials are closed under subtraction, the numerator is also a polynomial. So, the expression is a ratio of polynomials and is therefore a rational expression.

Sum of two cubic polynomials

The sum of two cubic polynomials is not necessarily a cubic polynomial. However, it is either a cubic polynomial or a polynomial of lesser degree. The sum of two cubic polynomials of the form $ax^3 + bx^2 + cx + d$, where $a \neq 0$, will have the same form, however it is possible that individual like terms are opposites and have a sum of 0. For example, the sum of $-3x^3 + 2x - 3$ and $3x^3 + 5x^2$ is $5x^2 + 2x - 3$, which is a quadratic polynomial. (Notice that coefficients b, c, and d in the cubic polynomial form are each allowed to equal zero; that is, cubic polynomials can be missing any of the terms with degree less than 3.)

Multiplying a binomial and a trinomial

To multiply a binomial and a trinomial, use the distributive property. Because a binomial has 2 terms and a trinomial has 3 terms, there will be $2 \cdot 3 = 6$ multiplications when multiplying the polynomials. In the example below, each term of the binomial is multiplied by the entire trinomial. Then, that multiplication is distributed to each term of the trinomial. In the final steps, like terms are combined and the answer is expressed in standard form, with terms written in order of descending degree.

$(x + 2)(x^2 - 3x + 9) = x(x^2 - 3x + 9) + 2(x^2 - 3x + 9) =$

$x^3 - 3x^2 + 9x + 2x^2 - 6x + 18 =$

$x^3 - x^2 + 3x + 18$

Remainder Theorem for polynomials

The Remainder Theorem for polynomials states that for a polynomial $P(x)$ and a real number a, the remainder when $P(x)$ is divided by $(x - a)$ is $P(a)$, the value of the polynomial evaluated at $x = a$. If there is no remainder, that is if the remainder equals 0, then $P(a) = 0$ and $(x - a)$ is a factor of the polynomial $P(x)$. For example, if $P(x) = (2x - 3)(3x + 1)$, this can be written as $P(x) = 6(x - \frac{3}{2})(x + \frac{1}{3})$. Here $P\left(\frac{3}{2}\right) = 0$ and $P\left(\frac{1}{3}\right) = 0$, so that the remainder is zero when $P(x)$ is divided by $(x - \frac{3}{2})$ and $(x + \frac{1}{3})$; $(x - \frac{3}{2})$ and $(x + \frac{1}{3})$ are therefore factors of $P(x)$.

On the other hand, the Remainder Theorem also can be used to obtain the remainder when the above $P(x)$ is divided by any binomial, such as $(x - 4)$:

$$Rem\left[\frac{P(x)}{x - 4}\right] = P(4) = (2(4) - 3)(3(4) + 1) = (8 - 3)(12 + 1) = 5 \cdot 13 = 65$$

Polynomial identity

A polynomial identity refers to two polynomials that can be shown equivalent by factoring, multiplying, or simplifying. For any value or values of the variables in the two polynomials, the values of the expressions will be identical. For example, the difference of squares formula $a^2 - b^2 = (a + b)(a - b)$ is a polynomial identity. The left side can be factored to obtain the right side, and/or the right side can be multiplied to obtain the left side. For any real numbers a and b, $a^2 - b^2$ yields the same result as $(a + b)(a - b)$.

Binomial Theorem for expanding the power of a binomial

The Binomial Theorem gives the expansion of the expression $(x + y)^n$, where x and y are real numbers and n is a positive integer. In other words, it gives a way to write each of the terms of the polynomial that results when $(x + y)$ is written as a multiplicative factor n times. The theorem can be written as follows:

$$(x + y)^n = a_0 x^n y^0 + a_1 x^{n-1} y^1 + a_2 x^{n-2} y^2 + \cdots + a_{n-1} x^1 y^{n-1} + a_n x^0 y^n$$

where the coefficients $a_0, a_1, ..., a_n$, are given by the $(n + 1)$th row of Pascal's Triangle. Pascal's Triangle is shown below up to $n = 4$, and the pattern continues such that each entry is the sum of the two entries diagonally above it.

$$1$$
$$1 \quad 1$$
$$1 \quad 2 \quad 1$$
$$1 \quad 3 \quad 3 \quad 1$$

Long division for polynomials

Long division for polynomials is similar to long division of integers. For example, when dividing 385 by 12, you first determine how many times 12 goes into 38 (and write 3 as the corresponding digit of the quotient). Then you subtract 36 from 38, giving 2, and the 5 is brought down to form 25, and so on. With polynomial division, the first term written for the quotient is equal to the first term of the dividend divided by the first term of the divisor. For example, if $5x^2 + 10x + 3$ is being divided by $x - 2$, the first term for the quotient is $\frac{5x^2}{x} = 5x$. $5x$ times $x - 2$ is $5x^2 - 10x$, and then $5x^2 - 10x$ is subtracted from $5x^2 + 10x$, yielding $20x$; the 3 is then brought down to form $20x + 3$. This process continues until the remainder is determined.

Polynomials are not closed under division

Polynomials are additions, subtractions and/or multiplication (but not division by variables) of variable expressions containing only non-negative integer exponents. To prove that polynomials are not closed under division, use a counterexample. Assume that polynomials are closed under

- 69 -

division. This means the quotient $(x + 1) \div x = \frac{x+1}{x} = 1 + \frac{1}{x} = 1 + x^{-1}$ would have to be a polynomial. This expression, however, is not a polynomial, because the term x^{-1} contains a negative exponent (or would have to be written as the division by x). All terms of a polynomial must be of the form ax^n, where a is a real number and n is a non-negative integer. Although there are *some* quotients of polynomials that are polynomials, closure requires this to be true for *all* polynomials.

Radical Expressions and Equations

Vertical asymptotes of a rational function

The vertical asymptotes of a rational function occur wherever the function is undefined, which is wherever the denominator of the function equals zero and the numerator does not equal zero. To find the vertical asymptotes, we simply find the zeros of the denominator, and eliminate any that are also zeros of the numerator (we can perform this check easily by simply plugging each one into the numerator to see if it causes the numerator to equal zero.) A rational function can therefore have as many vertical asymptotes as the degree of its denominator, but may have fewer.

Horizontal or oblique asymptotes of a rational function

Horizontal or slant asymptotes are the lines that the function may approach as its x-values approach infinity. A rational function can have at most one horizontal or oblique asymptote.

If the degree of the numerator is less than the degree of the denominator, the function has a horizontal asymptote at $y = 0$. If the degree of the numerator equals the degree of the denominator, the function has a horizontal asymptote at $y = c$, where c is the quotient of the highest-degree terms of the numerator and denominator (For example, if the leading term of the numerator is $5x^3$ and the leading term of the denominator is $2x^3$, the asymptote is at $y = \frac{5}{2}$.)

If the degree of the numerator is one greater than the degree of the denominator, then long division must be performed to simplify the entire fraction, and the resulting linear equation is the equation of the slant asymptote.

If the degree of the numerator exceeds the degree of the denominator by more than one, there is no horizontal or slant asymptote.

Example problems

Problem 1

State the domain and range of the function $y = \sqrt{x - 3} + 1$

> The domain of a basic square root function is the set of all real numbers greater than or equal to zero. That is because taking the square root of a negative number is not permitted. However, in this function we can see that values of x between 0 and 3 will also result in taking the square root of a negative number, and thus those values must also not be part of the domain. The function's domain is therefore the set of all real numbers greater than or equal to 3.

> Since square roots must always be positive, the range of a basic square root function is also the set of all real numbers greater than or equal to zero. In this case, however, the output values of the square root function will all have 1 added to them, so the final value of the function will never be less than 1. The function's range is therefore the set of all real numbers greater than or equal to 1.

Problem 2

Solve the equation $2\sqrt{x^2 - 5} + 3 = 7$ for x.

First it is necessary to isolate the square root sign on one side of the equation. Subtracting 3 from both sides and then dividing by 2 gives us $\sqrt{x^2 - 5} = 2$.

Squaring both sides is the next step: $x^2 - 5 = 4$.

Next, adding 5 to both sides yields $x^2 = 9$. This means that x can equal 3 or -3. However, squaring both sides of an equation can introduce extraneous solutions, so each of these solutions needs to be checked in the original equation. In this case, however, both solutions do check out, as they both yield $2\sqrt{9 - 5} + 3 = 7$.

Problem 3

If y varies directly with x and inversely with $z - x$, for what values of x and z does y have a nonzero value? Does this answer change if y varies directly with $z - x$ and inversely with x?

If y varies directly with x and inversely with $z - x$, the equation that expresses this variation is $= \frac{kx}{z-x}$, where k is a nonzero constant. This equation will be undefined whenever the denominator of the fraction equals zero (hence whenever $z = x$), and will equal zero whenever the numerator equals zero (hence whenever $x = 0$). At all other times, y will have a nonzero value.

If y varies directly with $z - x$ and inversely with x, the equation expresses this variation is $= \frac{k(z-x)}{x}$. This equation will be undefined whenever $x = 0$ and will equal zero whenever $z = x$; in other words, it will be undefined at all the points where the previous function equaled zero, and will equal zero at all the points where the previous function was undefined. At all other points, y will have a nonzero value, just as with the previous equation.

Problem 4

Find the asymptotes of the function $\frac{2x^2-2}{x^2+3x-4}$.

Vertical asymptotes occur wherever the denominator, but not the numerator, equals zero. The zeros of the denominator are -4 and 1; the zeros of the numerator are -1 and 1. Therefore, there is a vertical asymptote at $x = -4$, but not at $x = 1$ (Simplifying the fraction makes it clear why: the factor $(x - 1)$ simply cancels out.)

The numerator and denominator have the same degree. This means that to find the horizontal asymptote, we find the quotient of the leading terms of the numerator and denominator. $\frac{2x^2}{x^2}$ equals 2, so the function has a horizontal asymptote at $y = 2$.

Problem 5

The high school science club raised $240 from its members to pay the cost of a chartered bus for a field trip, with each member contributing an equal share. When four members of the club were unable to go on the trip, their money was refunded and each other member had to contribute an extra $2 to cover the bus cost. How many members does the club have?

If we let x equal the number of members, then we know that each member originally paid $\frac{240}{x}$ dollars. We also know that the same cost of $240 was covered by $x - 4$ members each paying $\frac{240}{x} + 2$ dollars. So we can write the equation $(x - 4)\left(\frac{240}{x} + 2\right) = 240$ and solve for x.

First, multiplying the terms out gives us $240 + 2x - \frac{960}{x} - 8 = 240$, which simplifies to $2x - \frac{960}{x} - 8 = 0$. If we isolate the fraction on one side $(2x - 8 = \frac{960}{x})$, then we can multiply both sides by x to clear fractions: $x(2x - 8) = 960$. From there we get the quadratic $2x^2 - 8x - 960 = 0$, which we can solve to get x = -20 and x = 24. 24 is therefore the number of students in the club.

- 73 -

Quadratic Equations

Number of solutions of a quadratic equation and it's graph

Each real solution of an equation represents a place where the graph of the equation crosses the x-axis. A parabolic graph can cross the x-axis in up to two places, just as a quadratic equation can have up to two real solutions. If the equation has two real solutions, the graph crosses the x-axis in the two places with x-coordinates equal to the two solutions. If the equation has one solution, the vertex of the graph lies at the corresponding coordinate on the x-axis. If the equation has no real solutions, the graph lies entirely above or below the x-axis and does not cross it.

Solving a quadratic inequality of the form $ax^2 + bx + c > 0$ or $ax^2 + bx + c < 0$

We can solve a quadratic inequality either by graphing or by algebraic methods. To solve it by graphing, we graph the corresponding equation $y = ax^2 + bx + c$ as a dashed-line parabola. Then, we can shade either the area below the parabola to represent y-values less than $ax^2 + bx + c$, or above the parabola to represent y-values greater than $ax^2 + bx + c$. Whichever portion of the x-axis is within the region below the parabola represents the solution set of the inequality $ax^2 + bx + c > 0$; whichever portion is within the region above the parabola represents the solution set of the inequality $ax^2 + bx + c < 0$. To solve the inequality algebraically, we find the solutions to the equation $ax^2 + bx + c = 0$. The solution set of the inequality is either the set of values between those two solutions, or the set of values "outside of" those two solutions. To find out which set is correct, we choose an x-value from one of those sets and determine if it makes the inequality true. If so, that set is the solution; if not, the other set is the solution.

Conic sections

There are four basic types of conic section: parabolas, hyperbolas, ellipses, and circles. A parabola is created when a plane intersects a cone at an angle parallel to one side of the cone. A hyperbola is created when a plane intersects a cone at an angle steeper than the side of the cone. The plane always intersects both halves of the cone in this case. An ellipse is created when a plane intersects a cone at an angle shallower than the side of the cone. This creates a closed curve. A circle is a special type of ellipse. It is created when the intersecting plane is parallel to the base of the cone.

Changing h, k, and r for a circle in the Cartesian plane

A circle in the Cartesian plane has the equation $(x - h)^2 + (y - k)^2 = r^2$. The constants h and k represent horizontal and vertical translations of the graph. The center of the circle will be k units above and h units to the right of the origin. Increasing h will move it further to the right and increasing k will move it further up; decreasing either of those constants will have the opposite effect, moving the graph down or to the left. The constant r represents the radius of the circle. Increasing r will make the circle larger and decreasing it will make the circle smaller. All three of these constants are independent of each other; changing two of them at once will, for example, move the circle up and to the left, or move it down and make it smaller, just as if those changes had been made separately.

Standard forms of the equations for a circle, ellipse, parabola, and hyperbola

The standard form for a circle is $x^2 + y^2 = a^2$. The constant a represents the radius of the circle.

The standard form for an ellipse is $\frac{x^2}{a^2} + \frac{y^2}{b^2} = 1$. The constants a and b represent the lengths of the axes.

The standard form for a parabola is $y^2 = 4ax$, or $x^2 = 4ay$. The constant a represents the x- or y-coordinate of the focus.

The standard form for a hyperbola is $\frac{x^2}{a^2} - \frac{y^2}{b^2} = 1$. The constants a and b determine the asymptotes of the hyperbola.

Relationship between graphs of an ellipse and a hyperbola

For the graphs of an ellipse and a hyperbola with the equations $\frac{x^2}{a^2} + \frac{y^2}{b^2} = 1$ and $\frac{x^2}{a^2} - \frac{y^2}{b^2} = 1$ respectively, assuming the same values of a and b for both graphs, the constant a represents the length of the semi major axis of both the ellipse and the hyperbola. This means that the hyperbola's closest points to the origin, the points $(a, 0)$ and $(-a, 0)$, are also the ellipse's farthest points from the origin, and the ellipse and hyperbola are tangent to each other at these two points.

The constant b represents the length of the semi minor axis of the ellipse, and also is the vertical distance from the vertices of the hyperbola to its asymptotes. This means that if a rectangle were drawn between the points (a, b), $(-a, b)$, $(a, -b)$, and $(-a, -b)$, the rectangle would be circumscribed about the ellipse, and the asymptotes of the hyperbola would pass through the corners of the rectangle.

Changing the constants in a quadratic equation of the form y = a(x – h)² + k

The constant a affects the width of the parabola; increasing a makes it narrower and decreasing a makes it wider. This means that increasing a will decrease the distance between the x-intercepts of the graph, and vice versa. The constants h and k represent the coordinates of the parabola's vertex. Increasing h will move the entire parabola to the right and decreasing h will move it to the left; increasing k will move it up and decreasing k will move it down. Moving the parabola to the right or left will move the x-intercepts right or left by the same distance. Moving it up or down can decrease or increase the number of x-intercepts by moving the parabola until it no longer intersects the x-axis (or until it does, if it did not before). Only when k equals zero will the parabola have exactly one x-intercept.

Relationship between the functions y = x² and $y = \sqrt{x}$

At first glance, it may seem that these functions are simply inverses of each other. However, the range of the square root function is limited in a way the domain of the square function is not. The square root function can't take on any positive y-values, so the positive x-values of the square function don't have any corresponding points to map to. Graphically, if the function $y = x^2$ were flipped about the line $y = x$, it would be a sideways parabola, which does not pass the vertical line test and so is not a function. The square root function $y = \sqrt{x}$ actually corresponds to just the top half of this sideways parabola. It could be said that $y = \sqrt{x}$ is the inverse of *half* of the function $y = x^2$: the half to the right of the y-axis.

Example problems

<u>Problem 1</u>

Describe how to find the domain and range of a quadratic function of the form $y = ax^2 + bx + c$.

> A quadratic function of the form described always has a domain that includes all real numbers. To find the range of the function, find the vertex of the parabolic graph and determine whether the parabola opens up or down.
>
> To find the vertex, first find the x-coordinate, which always has the value $\frac{-b}{2a}$. Plug this value into the original equation to find the corresponding y-coordinate.
>
> The sign of the x^2-coefficient a determines whether the parabola is concave up or down. If it is positive, the graph is concave up; if it is negative, the graph is concave down.
>
> If the graph is concave up, the range of the function consists of all y-values greater than or equal to the y-coordinate of the vertex; if the graph is concave down, the range of the function consists of all y-values less than or equal to the y-coordinate of the vertex.
>
> For example, if the vertex is at $(3, 7)$ and the graph is concave down, the range of the function is the set of all y-values less than or equal to 7.

<u>Problem 2</u>

The quadratic equation $4x^2 + bx + 9 = 0$ has only one solution. Find the solution.

> For a quadratic equation to have only one solution, its discriminant ($b^2 - 4ac$) must equal zero. In this case, we are given the values of a and c, so we can set $b^2 - 4ac$ equal to zero and solve for b:
>
> $$b^2 - 4ac = 0$$
>
> $$b^2 - 4(4)(9) = 0$$
>
> $$b^2 - 144 = 0$$
>
> $$b^2 = 144$$
>
> $$b = 12$$
>
> Then we can use the quadratic formula to find the solution of the equation. Since we already know that the discriminant equals zero, the equation $x = \frac{-b \pm \sqrt{b^2 - 4ac}}{2a}$ reduces to simply $x = \frac{-b}{2a}$. Substituting 12 for b and 4 for a gives us $x = \frac{-12}{8} = \frac{-3}{2}$.

Problem 3

The quadratic equation $y = ax^2 + 2x - 8$ has -2 as one of its roots. Find the other root.

Based on the root we know, we can determine the missing coefficient a in the quadratic equation. We plug in -2 for x and 0 for y, and solve for a:

$$0 = a(-2)^2 + 2(-2) - 8$$

$$0 = 4a - 4 - 8$$

$$0 = 4a - 12$$

$$4a = 12$$

$$a = 3.$$

Then we can find the other root by using the quadratic equation or by factoring. Factoring is easier since we already know one root: the factors are either $(3x + 2)(x + k)$ or $(3x + k)(x + 2)$. Since one root is x=-2, the other root must be $(3x+k)=0$. Trial and error tells us that k = -4, thus $\frac{4}{3}$ is the other root of the equation. We can check this by plugging it in as we did -2 above.

Problem 4

Find the x-coordinate of the vertex for a quadratic equation with the following values:

X	-1	0	1	2	3	4	5
Y	13	5	1	1	5	13	25

One way to find the approximate location of the vertex is by graphing the points in the table, sketching the parabola, and attempting to eyeball the vertex. Another way to find the vertex would be to find the equation of the parabola based on the points in the table, and then convert the equation to vertex form. However, analyzing the values in the table can tell us where the x-coordinate of the vertex is without needing to find the equation or graph it. The y-values are the same for x-values 1 and 2 (as well as for 0 and 3, and for -1 and 4), so the graph of the parabola is symmetric about the line x = 1.5. The vertex must lie on this line of symmetry, so the vertex has x-coordinate 1.5.

Problem 5

Find a quadratic equation whose real roots are x = 2 and x = -1.

One way to find the roots of a quadratic equation is to factor the equation and use the zero product property, setting each factor of the equation equal to zero to find the corresponding root. We can use this technique in reverse to find an equation given its roots. Each root corresponds to a linear equation which in turn corresponds to a factor of the quadratic equation.

For example, the root x = 2 corresponds to the equation x – 2 = 0, and the root x = -1 corresponds to the equation x + 1 = 0. These two equations correspond to the

- 77 -

factors $(x - 2)$ and $(x + 1)$, from which we can derive the equation $(x - 2)(x + 1) = 0$, or $x^2 - x - 2 = 0$.

(Any integer multiple of this entire equation will also yield the same roots, as the integer will simply cancel out when the equation is factored. For example, $2x^2 - 2x - 4 = 0$ factors as $2(x - 2)(x + 1) = 0$.)

Problem 6

A parabolic graph is concave down, has a y-intercept of -5, and has no x-intercepts. What can be determined about the equation of the graph?

The equation of a parabola is a quadratic, written in standard form as $y = ax^2 + bx + c$. Since the graph in this case is concave down, the x^2-coordinate a must be negative, though we do not know exactly what it is. We also know that the constant term, c, is equal to the y-intercept, in this case -5 (We can confirm this algebraically: no matter what a and b are, plugging the coordinates $(0, -5)$ into the equation gives us $-5 = c$.).

Finally, the lack of x-intercepts tells us that the equation has no real roots, so its discriminant, $b^2 - 4ac$, must be negative. Plugging in -5 for c means that the expression $b^2 + 20a$ is negative. We already know that b^2 must be positive (because it is the square of a real number), so now we also know that $-20a$ must be greater than b^2. This puts a limit on the possible values of a and b, even though we still do not know either of them exactly.

Problem 7

A parabolic graph intersects the x-axis at 1 and 3 and the y-axis at -6. What can be determined about the equation of the graph?

We can determine the entire equation of the graph from these three points. First of all, we know that the solutions of the equation are described by the quadratic formula: $x = \frac{-b \pm \sqrt{b^2 - 4ac}}{2a}$. We also know that c is equal to the y-intercept, which is -6, and we know that the vertex of the equation is midway between the x-intercepts, and its x-coordinate is $\frac{-b}{2a}$. So $\frac{-b}{2a} = 2$, meaning that $b = -4a$.

Substituting $-4a$ for b and -6 for c in the quadratic formula gives us $x = \frac{4a \pm \sqrt{16a^2 + 24a}}{2a}$, which reduces to $x = 2 \pm \frac{\sqrt{4a^2 + 6a}}{a}$. We know that the roots of this equation are 1 and 3, which equal 2 ± 1, so $\frac{\sqrt{4a^2 + 6a}}{a}$ must equal 1 or -1. Solving for a, we find $a = -2$. This means that $b = 8$, so the equation of the graph is $y = -2x^2 + 8x - 6$.

Problem 8

The graph of the equation $y = x^2 + 5x - 6$ is translated twelve units upward. What are the x-intercepts of the new graph?

Translating a graph upward simply adds the corresponding number to the constant term of the equation. Moving this graph upward twelve units means we add 12 to the constant term -6, so it becomes 6.

- 78 -

Now we must find the roots of the new equation $y = x^2 + 5x + 6$. We can do this through the quadratic equation or by factoring. As it happens, this equation factors handily: $(x + 2)(x +3)$ thus the roots of the equation are -2 and -3.

(Notice that these are unrelated to the roots of the original equation, which are 1 and -6.)

Problem 9

The graph of the equation $y = x^2 + 2x - 8$ is translated three units to the left. What are the x-intercepts of the new graph?

There is no simple algebraic transformation representing a horizontal shift of a parabolic graph. We could represent it by substituting $(x + 3)$ for x in the original equation (yielding $y = (x+3)^2 + 2(x+3) - 8$ or $y = x^2 + 8x +7$) and then simplifying. However, this isn't actually necessary, since all we need to find are the x-intercepts. The x-intercepts of the new graph will simply be the x-intercepts of the old graph shifted three units to the left. Finding the roots of the original equation is simple: the equation factors as $(x - 2)(x + 4)$, so the x-intercepts are at 2 and -4. Therefore, the x-intercepts of the shifted graph will be at $(2 - 3)$ and $(-4 - 3)$, or -1 and -7.

Problem 10

A swimming pool is 11 feet longer than it is wide. The area of the pool is 276 square feet. What are the dimensions of the pool?

If the width of the pool is x feet, the length is $x + 11$ and the area is therefore $x(x + 11) = x^2 + 11x$ square feet. We therefore have the quadratic equation $x^2 + 11x = 276$, or $x^2 + 11x - 276 = 0$.

Solving this equation gives us two possible values for x: 12 and -23. It does not make sense for the width of the pool to be -23 feet, so it must be 12 feet. Therefore, the length is $12 + 11 = 23$ feet. Checking this answer, we find that indeed, 12 times 23 is 276 square feet.

Problem 11

Find the vertex of the parabola whose equation is $y = x^2 + 2x - 15$ by translating the equation into the form $y = a(x - h)^2 + k$.

The coefficient of x^2 in the original equation equals 1, so that is the value of a in the new equation. The remaining constants are then found by completing the square. The value of h is found by taking the opposite of half of the x-coefficient, so h = -1. $1(x + 1)^2$ expands to $x^2 + 2x + 1$, and we need to find the value of k to add to this expression to make it equal $x^2 + 2x - 15$; that value is therefore -16. So the final form of the equation is $y = (x + 1)^2 - 16$. The coordinates of the vertex are (h, k), so the vertex is at (-1, 16).

Problem 12

One square picture frame has an area of 31 square inches less than twice the area of another square frame. If the second frame has an area of x square inches, write an expression for the side length of

- 79 -

the first frame. Then find the side lengths of the two frames given that the second is 3 inches shorter than the first.

The first frame's area is 31 less than twice x, or $2x - 31$. Its side length is therefore $\sqrt{2x - 31}$.

The side length of the second frame is $\sqrt{x}$, so an equation relating the two side lengths is $\sqrt{x} + 3 = \sqrt{2x - 31}$.

Since one side of the equation is a radical, we can start by squaring both sides: $x + 6\sqrt{x} + 9 = 2x - 31$.

Then we need to isolate the other radical so we can square both sides again. Subtracting both x and 9 from both sides leaves $6\sqrt{x} = x - 40$; and squaring leaves $36x = x^2 - 80x + 1600$.

Finally, we subtract $36x$ from both sides, giving us $x^2 - 116x + 1600 = 0$, and then solve for x: $x = 16$ or $x = 100$. So the second picture frame is either 4×4 inches (making the first frame 1×1) or 10×10 inches (making the first frame 13×13). Since we were told that the second frame is smaller than the first, the second answer is correct.

Problem 13

Find the inverse of the function

$$y = \frac{1}{2}\sqrt{2x + 6} - 1.$$

To find the inverse of a function, we switch the independent and dependent variables and then solve for y. In this case, we start with $x = \frac{1}{2}\sqrt{2y + 6} - 1$, add 1 to both sides, and multiply by 2, yielding $2x + 2 = \sqrt{2y + 6}$.

Now that we have isolated the square root, we can square both sides, giving us $(2x + 2)^2 = 2y + 6$. Expanding the left side gives us $4x^2 + 8x + 4 = 2y + 6$, and then we can isolate y by subtracting 6 from both sides and dividing through by 2. This gives us $y = 2x^2 + 4x - 1$.

Set Theory

Permutation

For each set of data, the individual elements may be arranged in different groups containing different numbers of elements arranged in different orders. For example, given the set of integers from one to three, inclusive, the elements of the set are 1, 2, and 3. They may be arranged as follows: 1, 2, 3, 12, 21, 13, 31, 23, 32, 123, 132, 231, 213, 312, and 321. These ordered sequences of elements from the given set of data are called permutations. It is important to note that in permutations, the order of the elements in the sequence is important. The sequence 123 is not the same as the sequence 213. Also, no element in the given set may be used more times as an element in a permutation than it appears as an element in the original set. For example, 223 is not a permutation in the above example because the number 2 only appears one time in the given set.

Number of permutations of a given set

The number of possible permutations of n items from a set of n items is $n!$, or $n(n-1)(n-2)(n-3)\ldots(3)(2)(1)$. To find the number of permutations of r items from a set of n items, use the formula ${}_nP_r = \frac{n!}{(n-r)!}$. When using this formula, each element of r must be unique. Also, this assumes that different arrangements of the same set of elements yields different outcomes. For example, 123 is not the same as 321; order is important! If the set contains duplicates of one or more elements, the formula changes slightly to accommodate the duplicates. Use the formula $= \frac{n!}{n_1!n_2!\ldots n_k!}$, where P is the number of permutations, n is the total number of elements in the set, and n_1, n_2, and n_3 are the number of duplicates of an individual element.

Possible permutations of a set of unique items

To find the total number of possible permutations of a set of unique items, you must apply the permutation formulas multiple times. For example, to find the total number of possible permutations of the set 1, 2, 3, first apply the formula $P = n!$ as follows: $P = n! = 3! = 6$. This gives the number of permutations of the three elements when all three elements are used. To find the number of permutations when two of the three elements are used, use the formula

$${}_nP_r = \frac{n!}{(n-r)!}, \text{ where } n \text{ is 3 and } r \text{ is 2.}$$

$${}_nP_r = \frac{n!}{(n-r)!} \Rightarrow {}_3P_2 = \frac{3!}{(3-2)!} = \frac{6}{1} = 6$$

To find the number of permutations when one element is used, use the formula

$${}_nP_r = \frac{n!}{(n-r)!}, \text{ where } n \text{ is 3 and } r \text{ is 1.}$$

$${}_nP_r = \frac{n!}{(n-r)!} \Rightarrow {}_3P_1 = \frac{3!}{(3-1)!} = \frac{3!}{2!} = \frac{6}{2} = 3$$

Find the sum of the three formulas: $6 + 6 + 3 = 15$ total possible permutations.

Factorial of a number

The factorial of a positive integer is represented by the ! sign. The factorial of a number is the product of the number and all positive integers less than the number. For example, 3! (read "3 factorial") means $3 \cdot 2 \cdot 1 = 6$. The exception to the rule is the case of zero factorial. In this case, $0! = 1$. This makes sense if you consider the pattern of factorials:

$$4! = 4 \cdot 3 \cdot 2 \cdot 1 = 24;$$

$$3! = 3 \cdot 2 \cdot 1 = \frac{4!}{4} = 6;$$

$$2! = 2 \cdot 1 = \frac{3!}{3} = 2;$$

$$1! = \frac{2!}{2} = 1;$$

$$0! = \frac{1!}{1} = 1$$

Combinations

For each set of data, the individual elements may be arranged in different groups containing different numbers of elements arranged in different orders. For example, given the set of integers from one to three, inclusive, the elements of the set are 1, 2, and 3. They may be arranged as follows: 1, 2, 3, 12, 21, 13, 31, 23, 32, 123, 132, 231, 213, 312, and 321. Some of the arrangements contain the exact same elements as other arrangements and must be discarded to avoid duplicates. This leaves 1, 2, 3, 12, 13, 23, and 123. These sequences of unique combinations of elements from the given set of data are called combinations. No element in the given set may be used more times as an element in a combination than it appears as an element in the original set. For example, 223 is not a combination in the above example because the number 2 only appears one time in the given set.

Number of combinations in a set of elements

In a set containing n elements, the number of combinations of r items from the set can be found using the formula $_nC_r = \frac{n!}{r!(n-r)!}$. Notice the similarity to the formula for permutations. In effect, you are dividing the number of permutations by $r!$ to get the number of combinations, and the formula may be written $_nC_r = \frac{_nP_r}{r!}$. When finding the number of combinations, it is important to remember that the elements in the set must be unique, that is, there must not be any duplicate items, and that no item is used more than once in any given sequence.

Difference between permutations and combinations

The biggest difference between permutations and combinations is the ordering of the sequences. In permutations, different sequences of the same group of elements create different permutations. In combinations, different sequences of the same group of elements create the same combination. It is easy to get the two terms confused, especially since the terms are misused in the English language. For example, combination locks do not require a combination, but a permutation. If you enter the correct numbers in the wrong order, you have entered a correct combination, but an incorrect permutation, and the lock will not open.

Points, Lines, Angles, and Planes

Finding the center and radius of a circle

<u>Example problem</u>

Use completing the square to find the center and radius of a circle given by the polynomial equation:

$$x^2 + y^2 + 6x - 2y - 6 = 0$$

Rewrite the equation by grouping the x-terms and y-terms and moving the constant to the other side of the equation.

$$x^2 + y^2 + 6x - 2y - 6 = 0$$

$$(x^2 + 6x) + (y^2 - 2y) = 6$$

Prepare to complete the square by adding spaces in each set of parentheses and on the other side of the equation.

$$(x^2 + 6x + \_) + (y^2 - 2y + \_) = 6 + \_ + \_$$

For the x group: $\left(\frac{6}{2}\right)^2 = 3^2 = 9$ For the y group: $\left(\frac{2}{2}\right)^2 = 1^2 = 1$ Determine what is added to each group by dividing the middle coefficient by 2 and then squaring the result.

$$(x^2 + 6x + 9) + (y^2 - 2y + 1) = 6 + 9 + 1$$

Factor the groups and simplify the right side of the equation.

$$(x + 3)^2 + (y - 1)^2 = 16$$

Factor the groups and simplify the right side of the equation.

$$(x + 3)^2 + (y - 1)^2 = 16.$$

Identify h, k, and r.

$$x - h = x + 3 \rightarrow h = -3$$

$$y - k = y - 1 \rightarrow k = 1$$

$$r^2 = 16 \rightarrow r = 4$$

The center of the circle is (-3, 1), and the radius is 4.

Equation of a parabola

Example problems

Problem 1: Identify the equation of a parabola given a focus and directrix.

focus: (2,5) and directrix: $y = 1$

> A parabola is the set of points equidistant from a point called the focus and line called the directrix, which does not pass through the focus. A parabola curves around the focus and away from the directrix but intersects neither. The vertex (h, k) of the parabola lies on the parabola's line of symmetry, which passes through the focus and is perpendicular to the directrix.
>
> Identify the orientation of the parabola. Since the directrix is a horizontal line represented by the equation $y = 1$, the parabola is oriented vertically and can therefore be represented by the equation $4p(y - k) = (x - h)^2$, where (h, k) is the vertex of the parabola and $(h, k + p)$ is the focus of the parabola. The vertex is halfway between the focus and the directrix, so find the mean of the y-values in the focus and directrix to find the vertex: $\left(2, \frac{5+1}{2}\right) \rightarrow (2,3) = (h, k)$. The y-value of the focus, 5, is represented by $k + p$; $k = 3$, so $3 + p = 5 \rightarrow p = 2$. Substitute h, k, and p into the equation of a parabola: $4p(y - k) = (x - h)^2 \rightarrow 8(y - 3) = (x - 2)^2$.

Problem 2: Given a focus and directrix, identify the equation of a parabola.

focus: (6, −2) and directrix: $x = 0$

> A parabola is the set of points equidistant from a point called the focus and line called the directrix, which does not pass through the focus. A parabola curves around the focus and away from the directrix but intersects neither. The vertex (h, k) of the parabola lies on the parabola's line of symmetry, which passes through the focus and is perpendicular to the directrix.
>
> Identify the orientation of the parabola. Since the directrix is a vertical line represented by the equation $x = 0$, the parabola is oriented horizontally and can therefore be represented by the equation $4p(x - h) = (y - k)^2$, where (h, k) is the vertex of the parabola and $(h + p, k)$ is the focus of the parabola. The vertex is halfway between the focus and the directrix, so find the mean of the x-values in the focus and directrix to find the vertex: $\left(\frac{6+0}{2}, -2\right) \rightarrow (3, -2)$. Compare the x-values in the vertex and the focus to find p: $p = 6 - 3 = 3$. Substitute h, k, and p into the equation of a parabola: $4p(x - h) = (y - k)^2 \rightarrow 12(x - 3) = (y + 2)^2$.

Equation of an ellipse

Example problems

Problem 1: Identify the equation of an ellipse with foci at (5,3) and (11,3) and a focal constant of 10.

An ellipse is the set of points around two foci such that the sum of the distances from any point on the ellipse to each focus is the focal constant. The center of the ellipse is equidistant from the foci and lies on the major axis. The orientation of the ellipse is also along the major axis. The ends of the major axis are called vertices. The ends of the minor axis are called co-vertices. Identify the orientation of the ellipse. The y-values are the same in both foci, so the major axis of the ellipse is at $y = 3$. Therefore, the ellipse is oriented horizontally. The equation for an ellipse with a horizontal major axis is $\frac{(x-h)^2}{a^2} + \frac{(y-k)^2}{b^2} = 1$, where (h, k) is the he center of the ellipse, a is half the focal constant, and a and b are related by the equation $a^2 - b^2 = c^2$, where c is the horizontal distance between the focus and the center. The center is the point along the major axis between the two foci: $\left(\frac{11+5}{2}, 3\right) \rightarrow (8,3)$. Find the horizontal distance c between the focus and the center: $c = 11 - 8 = 3$. Divide the focal constant by 2 to find a: $a = \frac{10}{2} = 5$. Find b by using a, c, and the formula $a^2 - b^2 = c^2$: $5^2 - b^2 = 3^2 \rightarrow 25 - b^2 = 9 \rightarrow b^2 = 25 - 9 = 16 \rightarrow b = 4$. Substitute a, b, h, and k into the equation of an ellipse: $\frac{(x-h)^2}{a^2} + \frac{(y-k)^2}{b^2} = 1 \rightarrow$ $\frac{(x-8)^2}{5^2} + \frac{(y-3)^2}{4^2} = 1 \rightarrow \frac{(x-8)^2}{25} + \frac{(y-3)^2}{16} = 1$.

Problem 2: Identify the equation of an ellipse with foci at (2,1) and (2,5) and a focal constant of 5.

An ellipse is the set of points around two foci such that the sum of the distances from any point on the ellipse to each focus is the focal constant. The center of the ellipse is equidistant from the foci and lies on the major axis. The orientation of the ellipse is also along the major axis. The ends of the major axis are called vertices. The ends of the minor axis are called co-vertices. Identify the orientation of the ellipse. The x-values are the same in both foci, so the major axis of the ellipse is at $x = 2$. Therefore, the ellipse is oriented vertically. The equation for an ellipse with a horizontal major axis is $\frac{(x-h)^2}{b^2} + \frac{(y-k)^2}{a^2} = 1$, where (h, k) is the he center of the ellipse, a is half the focal constant, and a and b are related by the equation $a^2 - b^2 = c^2$, where c is the vertical distance between the focus and the center. The center is the point along the major axis between the two foci:: $\left(2, \frac{1+5}{2}\right) \rightarrow (2,3)$. Find the vertical distance c between the focus and the center: $c = 5 - 3 = 2$. Divide the focal constant by 2 to find a: $a = \frac{5}{2} = 2.5$. Find b by using a, c, and the formula $a^2 - b^2 = c^2$: $(2.5)^2 - b^2 = 2^2 \rightarrow 6.25 - b^2 = 4 \rightarrow b^2 = 6.25 - 4 = 2.25 \rightarrow b = 1.5$. Substitute a, b, h, and k into the equation of an ellipse: $\frac{(x-h)^2}{b^2} + \frac{(y-k)^2}{a^2} = 1 \rightarrow$ $\frac{(x-2)^2}{1.5^2} + \frac{(y-3)^2}{2.5^2} = 1 \rightarrow \frac{(x-2)^2}{2.25} + \frac{(y-3)^2}{6.25} = 1 \rightarrow \frac{(x-2)^2}{\frac{9}{4}} + \frac{(y-3)^2}{\frac{25}{4}} = 1 \rightarrow \frac{4(x-2)^2}{9} +$ $\frac{4(y-3)^2}{25} = 1$.

Equation of a hyperbola

Example problems

Problem 1: Identify the equation of a hyperbola given the foci $(-4,5)$ and $(6,5)$ and focal constant 8.

A hyperbola is the set of points whose distances from the foci are different by a constant (the focal constant). The foci are two points, one in each section of the hyperbola. The center, (h, k), is a point between the two sections of the hyperbola and is equidistant from the foci and along the major axis.

To find the equation of the hyperbola, first identify the orientation of the hyperbola. The foci lie along the line $y = 5$, so the hyperbola is orientated horizontally. The center is the point equidistant from the foci: $\left(\frac{-4+6}{2}, 5\right) \to (1,5)$. Compare the x-values of the center and one focus to find c: $c = 1 - (-4) = 5$. Divide the focal constant by 2 to find a: $a = \frac{8}{2} = 4$. Find b by using a, c, and the formula $a^2 + b^2 = c^2$: $4^2 + b^2 = 5^2 \to 16 + b^2 = 25 \to b^2 = 25 - 16 = 9 \to b = 3$. Substitute a, b, h, and k into the equation of a horizontally oriented hyperbola: $\frac{(x-h)^2}{a^2} - \frac{(y-k)^2}{b^2} = 1 \to \frac{(x-1)^2}{4^2} - \frac{(y-5)^2}{3^2} = 1 \to \frac{(x-1)^2}{16} - \frac{(y-5)^2}{9} = 1$.

Problem 2: Identify the equation of a hyperbola with foci at $(-2, -4)$ and $(-2, 22)$ and a focal constant of 10.

A hyperbola is the set of points whose distances from the foci are different by a constant (the focal constant). The foci are two points, one in each section of the hyperbola. The center, (h, k), is a point between the two sections of the hyperbola and is equidistant from the foci and along the major axis.

To find the equation of the hyperbola, first identify the orientation of the hyperbola. The foci lie along the line $x = -2$, so the hyperbola is orientated vertically. The center is the point equidistant from the foci: $\left(-2, \frac{-4+22}{2}\right) \to (-2,9)$. Compare the y-values of the center and one focus to find c: $c = 22 - 9 = 13$. Divide the focal constant by 2 to find a: $a = \frac{10}{2} = 5$. Find b by using a, c, and the formula $a^2 + b^2 = c^2$: $5^2 + b^2 = 13^2 \to 25 + b^2 = 169 \to b^2 = 169 - 25 = 144 \to b = 12$. Substitute a, b, h, and k into the equation of a vertically oriented hyperbola: $\frac{(y-k)^2}{a^2} - \frac{(x-h)^2}{b^2} = 1 \to \frac{(y-9)^2}{5^2} - \frac{(x+2)^2}{12^2} = 1 \to \frac{(y-9)^2}{25} - \frac{(x+2)^2}{144} = 1$.

Equation of a circle

Example problems

Problem 1: Derive the equation of a circle with a given center and radius using the Pythagorean Theorem.

Given is a circle with center (h, k) and radius r. Point (x, y) is on the circle. Use the Pythagorean Theorem to determine a relationship between the distance r and the points (h, k) and (x, y). In the right triangle, the length of the horizontal leg is $(x - h)$ and the length of the vertical leg is $(y - k)$. The Pythagorean Theorem states that

- 86 -

the square of the hypotenuse is equal to the sum of the squares of the legs, or $(x - h)^2 + (y - k)^2 = r^2$. This equation defines the circle with center (h, k), radius r, and point (x, y) on the circle.

Problem 2: Find the equation of a circle with center $(-2,8)$ and radius $r = 6$ using the Pythagorean Theorem.

Given a circle with center $(-2,8)$ and radius $r = 6$. Point (x, y) is on the circle.

Use the Pythagorean Theorem to determine a relationship between the distance $r = 6$ and the points $(-2,8)$ and (x, y). In the right triangle, the length of the horizontal leg is $(x + 2)$ and the length of the vertical leg is $(y - 8)$. The Pythagorean Theorem states that the square of the hypotenuse is equal to the sum of the squares of the legs, or $(x - h)^2 + (y - k)^2 = r^2 \rightarrow (x + 2)^2 + (y - 8)^2 = 6^2 \rightarrow (x + 2)^2 + (y - 8)^2 = 36$.

Determining whether a quadrilateral is a rectangle

Example problems

Problem 1: Determine whether or not the quadrilateral defined by $A(5,4)$, $B(-4,3)$, $C(-4,1)$, and $D(5,1)$ is a rectangle.

A rectangle has two pairs of congruent opposite sides and four right angles. To find the lengths of the sides, use the distance formula, $d = \sqrt{(x_1 - x_2)^2 + (y_1 - y_2)^2}$.

AB	BC
$\sqrt{[5 - (-4)]^2 + (4 - 3)^2}$	$\sqrt{[-4 - (-4)]^2 + (3 - 1)^2}$
$\sqrt{(9)^2 + (1)^2}$	$\sqrt{(0)^2 + (2)^2}$
$\sqrt{81 + 1}$	$\sqrt{0 + 4}$
$\sqrt{82}$	$\sqrt{4} = 2$
CD	DA
$\sqrt{(-4 - 5)^2 + (1 - 1)^2}$	$\sqrt{(5 - 5)^2 + (1 - 4)^2}$
$\sqrt{(-9)^2 + (0)^2}$	$\sqrt{(0)^2 + (-3)^2}$
$\sqrt{81 + 0}$	$\sqrt{0 + 9}$
$\sqrt{81} = 9$	$\sqrt{9} = 3$

Since AB $\neq$ CD and BC $\neq$ DA, Quadrilateral ABCD is not a rectangle, and no further testing is required.

Problem 2: Determine whether or not the quadrilateral defined by $A(8, -1)$, $B(-2, -1)$, $C(-2,6)$, and $D(8,6)$ is a rectangle.

A rectangle has 2 pairs of congruent opposite sides and 4 right angles. To find the lengths of the sides, use the distance formula, $d = \sqrt{(x_1 - x_2)^2 + (y_1 - y_2)^2}$.

AB	BC
$\sqrt{[8 - (-2)]^2 + [-1 - (-1)]^2}$	$\sqrt{[-2 - (-2)]^2 + (-1 - 6)^2}$
$\sqrt{(10)^2 + (0)^2}$ or $\sqrt{100 + 0}$	$\sqrt{(0)^2 + (-7)^2}$ o $\sqrt{0 + 49}$
$\sqrt{100} = 10$	$\sqrt{49} = 7$

- 87 -

CD	DA
$\sqrt{(-2-8)^2 + (6-6)^2}$	$\sqrt{(8-8)^2 + [6-(-1)]^2}$
$\sqrt{(-10)^2 + (0)^2}$ or	$\sqrt{(0)^2 + (7)^2}$ or $\sqrt{0 + 49}$
$\sqrt{100 + 0}$	$\sqrt{49} = 7$
$\sqrt{100} = 10$	

Since AB = CD & BC = DA, Test to see if quadrilateral ABCD is a rectangle. To find if the angles are right angles, find the slopes of the four sides. Perpendicular sides will have opposite, inverse slopes.

$\underline{AB}$	$m = \frac{(-1)-(-1)}{(-2)-8} = \frac{0}{-10} = 0$	$\underline{BC}$	$m = \frac{6-(-1)}{(-2)-(-2)} = \frac{7}{0} = undef$
$\underline{CD}$	$m = \frac{6-6}{8-(-2)} = \frac{0}{10} = 0$	$\underline{DA}$	$m = \frac{(-1)-6}{(-2)-(-2)} = \frac{-7}{0} = undef$

Although $\overline{BC}$ and $\overline{DA}$ have undefined slopes, they are perpendicular to $\overline{AB}$ and $\overline{CD}$ because lines with undefined slopes are perpendicular to lines with slopes of 0.

Point on a circle

Example problems

Problem 1: Determine whether or not the point $(3, 3\sqrt{3})$ lies on the circle which is centered at the origin and which contains the point $(0,6)$.

A circle consists of all points in a plane that are a given distance from the center. One way to determine whether a point lies on a particular circle is to find the distance between the center of the circle and the point, and compare it to the radius of the circle. If they are the same, then the point lies on the circle.

Begin by finding the radius of the circle:

$$r = \sqrt{(6-0)^2 + (0-0)^2} = \sqrt{36} = 6$$

If the point $(3, 3\sqrt{3})$ is also 6 units from the circle's center, then it lies on the circle.

$$d = \sqrt{(3-0)^2 + \left(3\sqrt{3} - 0\right)^2} = \sqrt{9 + 27} = \sqrt{36} = 6$$

Therefore, point $(3, 3\sqrt{3})$ lies on the given circle.

Problem 2: Determine whether or not the point $(1,2)$ lies on the circle which is centered at the origin and which contains the point $(\sqrt{2}, \sqrt{2})$.

A circle consists of all points in a plane that are a given distance from the center. One way to determine whether a point lies on a particular circle is to find the distance between the center of the circle and the point, and compare it to the radius of the circle. If they are the same, then the point lies on the circle.

Begin by finding the radius of the circle:

$$r = \sqrt{\left(\sqrt{2} - 0\right)^2 + \left(\sqrt{2} - 0\right)^2} = \sqrt{2 + 2} = \sqrt{4} = 2$$

If the point (1,2) is also 2 units from the circle's center, then it lies on the circle.

$$d = \sqrt{(1-0)^2 + (2-0)^2} = \sqrt{1+4} = \sqrt{5} \neq 2$$

Therefore, point (1,2) does not lie on the given circle.

Using slope-intercept form

Example problems

Problem 1: Show that the lines given by equations $5y + 2x = 7$ and $10y + 4x = 28$ are parallel.

Parallel lines are two lines which have the same slope and do not intersect. To determine whether $5y + 2x = 7$ and $10y + 4x = 28$ are parallel, first find the slope of each line by rewriting in slope-intercept form: $5y = -2x + 7 \rightarrow y = \frac{-2}{5}x + \frac{7}{5}$; $10y = -4x + 28 \rightarrow y = \frac{-4}{10}x + \frac{28}{10} \rightarrow y = \frac{-2}{5}x + \frac{14}{5}$. The two lines have same slope. To show the lines do not intersect, show that there is no solution to the system formed by the given equations. $\frac{-2}{5}x + \frac{7}{5} = \frac{-2}{5}x + \frac{14}{5} \rightarrow \frac{7}{5} = \frac{14}{5}$. When the solution of a system of equations results in a false statement, the solution is the empty set; there is no point contained by both lines, so the lines do not intersect.

Problem 2: Show that the lines given by equations $y - 3x = 5$ and $3y + x = -6$ are perpendicular.

When two lines have slopes which are negative reciprocals of each other. ($m_1 \cdot m_2 = -1$), they are perpendicular, which means they meet at right angles.

Find the slope of the given two lines, $y - 3x = 5$ and $3y + x = -6$, by rewriting in slope-intercept form: $y = 3x + 5$; $3y = -x - 6 \rightarrow y = \frac{-1}{3}x - \frac{6}{3} \rightarrow y = \frac{-1}{3}x - 2$. The two lines have slopes $m_1 = 3$ and $m_2 = \frac{-1}{3}$, which are negative reciprocals. Therefore, the lines are perpendicular.

Problem 3: Find the equation of the line passing through $(-2,6)$ and parallel to $5y - 15x = -25$.

Parallel lines have the same slopes.

Given equation: $5y - 15x = -25$ $5y = 15x - 25$ $y = 3x - 5$ Slope: $m_1 = 3 = m_2$	Solution equation: $y = m \cdot x + b$ $(y = 6, m_2 = 3, x = -2)$ $6 = 3 \cdot (-2) + b$ $6 = -6 + b$ $12 = b$ ------------------------------ $y = 3x + 12$ $y - 3x = 12$

- 89 -

The line passing through $(-2,6)$ and parallel to $5y - 15x = -25$ is $y - 3x = 12$.

Problem 4: Find the equation of the line passing through $(9, -1)$ and perpendicular to $-2y + 3x = 5$.

Perpendicular lines have opposite, inverse slopes.

Given equation: $-2y + 3x = 5$	Solution equation: $y = m \cdot x + b$
$-2y = -3x + 5$ $\quad y = \dfrac{-3}{-2}x + 5$ $\quad y = \dfrac{3}{2}x + 5$ Slope: $m_1 = \dfrac{3}{2}$ $\quad m_1 \cdot m_2 = -1$ $\quad \dfrac{3}{2} \cdot m_2 = -1$ $\quad m_2 = \dfrac{-2}{3}$	$(y = -1, m_2 = \dfrac{-2}{3}, x = 9)$ $\quad -1 = \dfrac{-2}{3} \cdot 9 + b$ $\quad -1 = -6 + b$ $\quad 5 = b$ ---------------------------------- $\quad y = \dfrac{-2}{3} \cdot x + 5$ $\quad 3y = -2x + 15$ $\quad 3y + 2x = 15$

The line passing through $(9, -1)$ and perpendicular to $-2y + 3x = 5$ is $3y + 2x = 15$.

Point that partitions a line segment

Example problems

Problem 1: Describe how to find the point that partitions a given line segment into two segments with a given length ratio.

Given two points, (x_1, y_1) and (x_2, y_2) and the ratio $a{:}b$.

steps:	x-values:	y-values:
find the difference between the values	$d_x = x_2 - x_1$	$d_y = y_2 - y_1$
find the fraction that represents the ratio	$a{:}b \rightarrow \dfrac{a}{a+b}$ this is the fraction of difference between x_1 and x_3	$a{:}b \rightarrow \dfrac{a}{a+b}$ this is also the fraction of difference between y_1 and y_3
find the difference between the first point and the partition point, multiply the fraction and the differences between x_1 and x_2 and y_1 and y_2	$m = \dfrac{a}{a+b} \cdot d_x$	$n = \dfrac{a}{a+b} \cdot d_y$
find the partition point by adding the differences to the first point	$x_3 = x_1 + m$	$y_3 = y_1 + n$

Problem 2: Describe and execute the steps to find the point that partitions the line segment between $(3,4)$ and $(7,12)$ into two segments with a length ratio of $1:3$.

Given two points, $(3,4)$ and $(7,12)$ and ratio $1:3$.

steps:	x-values:	y-values:
find the difference between the values	$d_x = 7 - 3 = 4$	$d_y = 12 - 4 = 8$
find the fraction that represents the ratio	$1:3 \rightarrow \dfrac{1}{1+3} = \dfrac{1}{4}$ this is the fraction of difference between x_1 and x_3	$1:3 \rightarrow \dfrac{1}{1+3} = \dfrac{1}{4}$ this is also the fraction of difference between y_1 and y_3
find the difference between the first point and the partition point, multiply the fraction and the differences between x_1 and x_2 and y_1 and y_2	$m = \dfrac{1}{4} \cdot 4 = 1$	$n = \dfrac{1}{4} \cdot 8 = 2$
find the partition point by adding the differences to the first point	$x_3 = 3 + 1 = 4$	$y_3 = 4 + 2 = 6$

The partition point is $(4,6)$.

Problem 3: Describe and execute the steps to find the point that partitions the line segment between $(-3,5)$ and $(3,-7)$ into two segments with a length ratio of $5:1$.

Given two points, $(-3,5)$ and $(3,-7)$ and ratio $5:1$.

steps:	x-values:	y-values:
1. Find the difference between the values	$d_x = 3 - (-3) = 6$	$d_y = (-7) - 5 = -12$
2. Find the fraction that represents the ratio	$5:1 \rightarrow \dfrac{5}{5+1} = \dfrac{5}{6}$ this is the fraction of difference between x_1 & x_3	$5:1 \rightarrow \dfrac{5}{5+1} = \dfrac{5}{6}$ this is also the fraction of difference between y_1 and y_3
3. find the difference between the first point & the partition point, multiply the fraction & the differences between x_1 & x_2 & y_1 & y_2	$m = \dfrac{5}{6} \cdot 6 = 5$	$n = \dfrac{5}{6} \cdot (-12) = -10$
4. find the partition point by adding the differences to the first point	$x_3 = -3 + 5 = 2$	$y_3 = 5 + (-10) = -5$

The partition point is $(2,-5)$.

Using coordinates to find perimeter and area

To use coordinates to find the perimeter of a figure, find the distance between all vertices. Add all the distances together.

$$d_{AB} = \sqrt{(x_B - x_A)^2 + (y_B - y_A)^2}$$

To use coordinates to find the area of a figure, find the critical distances. Use the appropriate formula.

for TRIANGLES: find the *BASE* and the *HEIGHT* **the height may not be along the side of the triangle** use the formula: $AREA = \frac{1}{2} \cdot BASE \cdot HEIGHT$	for RECTANGLES: find the *LENGTH* and the *WIDTH* use the formula: $AREA = LENGTH \cdot WIDTH$

Example problems

Problem 1: Find the perimeter of the figure given by the points $A(5,4)$, $B(3,-1)$, and $C(7,-1)$.

$$d_{AB} = \sqrt{(3-5)^2 + (-1-4)^2} = \sqrt{(-2)^2 + (-5)^2} = \sqrt{4+25} = \sqrt{29}$$

$$d_{BC} = \sqrt{(7-3)^2 + [-1-(-1)]^2} = \sqrt{(4)^2 + (0)^2} = \sqrt{16+0} = \sqrt{16} = 4$$

$$d_{CA} = \sqrt{(5-7)^2 + [4-(-1)]^2} = \sqrt{(-2)^2 + (5)^2} = \sqrt{4+25} = \sqrt{29}$$

Perimeter: $d_{AB} + d_{BC} + d_{CA} = \sqrt{29} + 4 + \sqrt{29} = 4 + 2\sqrt{29}$.

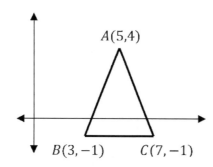

Problem 2: Find the perimeter of the figure given by the points $A(7,11)$, $B(3,3)$, $C(9,0)$ and $D(13,8)$.

$$d_{AB} = \sqrt{(3-7)^2 + (3-11)^2} = \sqrt{(-4)^2 + (-8)^2} = \sqrt{16+64} = \sqrt{80} = 4\sqrt{5}$$

$$d_{BC} = \sqrt{(9-3)^2 + (0-3)^2} = \sqrt{(6)^2 + (-3)^2} = \sqrt{36+9} = \sqrt{45} = 3\sqrt{5}$$

$$d_{CD} = \sqrt{(13-9)^2 + (8-0)^2} = \sqrt{(4)^2 + (8)^2} = \sqrt{16+64} = \sqrt{80} = 4\sqrt{5}$$

$$d_{DA} = \sqrt{(7-13)^2 + (11-8)^2} = \sqrt{(-6)^2 + (3)^2} = \sqrt{36+9} = \sqrt{45} = 3\sqrt{5}$$

Perimeter: $d_{AB} + d_{BC} + d_{CD} + d_{DA} = 4\sqrt{5} + 3\sqrt{5} + 4\sqrt{5} + 3\sqrt{5} = 2(4\sqrt{5}) + 2(3\sqrt{5}) = 8\sqrt{5} + 6\sqrt{5} = 14\sqrt{5}.$

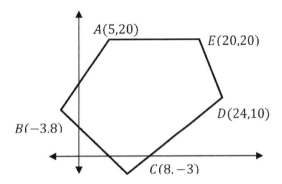

Problem 3: Find the area of the figure given by the points $A(5,4)$, $B(3,-1)$, and $C(7,-1)$.

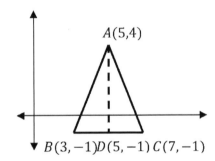

$BASE = d_{BC} = \sqrt{(7-3)^2 + [-1-(-1)]^2} = \sqrt{(4)^2 + (0)^2} = \sqrt{16 + 0} = \sqrt{16} = 4$

The _HEIGHT_ is the line segment through A and perpendicular to $\overline{BC}$.

$HEIGHT = d_{AD} = \sqrt{(5-5)^2 + (-1-4)^2} = \sqrt{(0)^2 + (-5)^2} = \sqrt{0 + 25} = \sqrt{25} = 5$

$AREA = \frac{1}{2} \cdot BASE \cdot HEIGHT = \frac{1}{2} \cdot 4 \cdot 5 = \frac{1}{2} \cdot 20 = 10$

The area of the triangle is 10 square units.

Problem 4: Find the area of the figure given by the points $A(7,11)$, $B(3,3)$, and $C(13,8)$.

$$BASE = d_{AC} = \sqrt{(13-7)^2 + (8-11)^2} = \sqrt{(6)^2 + (-3)^2} = \sqrt{36+9} = \sqrt{45} = 3\sqrt{5}$$

$$\overline{AC} \perp \overline{AB} \text{ because } m_{AB} \cdot m_{AC} = \frac{11-8}{7-13} \cdot \frac{11-3}{7-3} = \frac{3}{-6} \cdot \frac{8}{4} = \frac{24}{-24} = -1.$$

$$HEIGHT = d_{AB} = \sqrt{(3-7)^2 + (3-11)^2} = \sqrt{(-4)^2 + (-8)^2} = \sqrt{16+64} = \sqrt{80} = 4\sqrt{5}$$

$$AREA = \frac{1}{2} \cdot BASE \cdot HEIGHT = \frac{1}{2} \cdot 3\sqrt{5} \cdot 4\sqrt{5} = \frac{1}{2} \cdot 12 \cdot 5 =$$

$\frac{1}{2} \cdot 60 = 30$ The area of the triangle is 30 square units.

Problem 5: Find the area of the figure given by the points $A(7,11)$, $B(3,3)$, $C(9,0)$ and $D(13,8)$.

$$LENGTH = d_{AB} = \sqrt{(3-7)^2 + (3-11)^2} = \sqrt{(-4)^2 + (-8)^2} = \sqrt{16+64} = \sqrt{80} = 4\sqrt{5}$$

$$\overline{AB} \perp \overline{AD} \text{ because } m_{AB} \cdot m_{AD} = \frac{11-3}{7-3} \cdot \frac{11-8}{7-13} = \frac{8}{4} \cdot \frac{3}{-6} = \frac{24}{-24} = -1.$$

$$WIDTH = d_{AD} = \sqrt{(13-7)^2 + (8-11)^2} = \sqrt{(6)^2 + (-3)^2} =$$

$$\sqrt{36+9} = \sqrt{45} = 3\sqrt{5}$$

$$AREA = LENGTH \cdot WIDTH = 4\sqrt{5} \cdot 3\sqrt{5} = 12 \cdot 5 = 60$$

The area of the rectangle is 60 square units.

Point

A _point_ is a specific location and is used to help understand and define all other concepts in geometry. A point is denoted by a single capital letter, such as point P.

$\bullet$ P

Angle

An angle is the set of points which are part of two lines that intersect at a specific point. An angle is made up of two "half lines" called rays that begin at the shared point, called the vertex, and extend away from that point. An angle can be denoted simply by the angle's vertex ($\angle A$ or $\angle A$) or by three points: one from one ray, the point of intersection, and one from the second ray ($\angle BAC$ or $\angle BAC$).

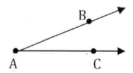

Circle

Circle – A continuous set of points which are all equidistant from a separate point called the center. A circle usually shares the same label as its center: circle P with center at point P.

Perpendicular lines

Perpendicular lines – Two lines which intersect at one specific point and create four 90° angles. Notation: $\overleftrightarrow{DE} \perp \overleftrightarrow{EF}$ when lines DE and EF intersect and form right angles at point E.

Parallel lines

Parallel lines – Two lines which do not share any points and never intersect. Notation: $\overleftrightarrow{GH} \parallel \overleftrightarrow{IJ}$.

Line segment

Line segment – The section of a line that is between two specific points on that line, usually denoted by two points: $\overline{KL}$.

Respresenting transformations

Transparencies

After drawing a shape on a piece of transparency, the shape can be rotated by leaving the transparency on a flat surface and turning it clockwise or counterclockwise.

After drawing a shape on a piece of transparency, the shape can be translated by leaving the transparency on a flat surface and sliding it in any direction (left, right, up, down, or along a diagonal).

After drawing a shape on a piece of transparency, the shape can be reflected by turning the transparency over so that the side the shape is on the underside of the transparency, touching the table.

Functions to represent a translation on the Cartesian plane

First, determine the points which define the shape. Second, use an equation or equations to express how the vertices of the shape are moving. When the shape is translated both vertically and horizontally, the translation can be expressed using two equations: one for the x-values and one for the y-values.

For example, consider a triangle, which is defined by its vertices at three specific ordered pairs. Adding 5 to each of the x-values will create a second triangle five units to the right of the first triangle; the equation representing this transformation is $x_2 = x_1 + 5$, where x_1 represents the x-coordinates of the original triangle and x_2 represents the x-coordinates of the translated triangle. If the triangle is also moved four units downward, the equation $y_2 = y_1 - 4$ can be used to find the new y=coordinates, represented by y_2, from the triangle's original y-coordinates, represented by y_1. Together, the horizontal and vertical shift can be written as $\begin{cases} x_2 = x_1 + 5 \\ y_2 = y_1 - 4 \end{cases}$, and these equations would be used to transform each vertex like so:

first point (x_1, y_1)	first vertex (3,6)
x-values: $x_2 = x_1 + 5$	$x_2 = 3 + 5 = 8$
y-values: $y_2 = y_1 - 4$	$y_2 = 6 - 4 = 2$

new point (x_2, y_2)	first vertex (8,2)
second vertex (5,1)	third vertex (4, −1)
$x_2 = 5 + 5 = 10$	$x_2 = 4 + 5 = 9$
$y_2 = 1 − 4 = −3$	$y_2 = −1 − 4 = −5$
second vertex (10, −3)	third vertex (9, −5)

Size and shape when translated or stretched horizontally

When a figure is translated, it moves to another location within the plane; since each point is shifted by the same distance, its size and shape remain the same. When a figure is stretched horizontally, its size and shape are affected. For example, consider an equilateral triangle which has a horizontal base. If the two endpoints of the base are pulled horizontally in opposite directions, the angle opposite the base widens as the two other angles become smaller. So, the lengths of the sides and the angle measures change, and the resulting triangle differs in both size and shape from the original triangle.

Transformations that carry a figure onto itself

Rectangle

A rectangle will be carried onto itself when it is rotated any multiple of 180° either clockwise or counterclockwise about its center. If the rectangle is a square, a rotation of 90° or any multiple of 90° clockwise or counterclockwise about the center will carry the square onto itself.

Any rectangle will be carried onto itself when it is rotated 360° or any multiple of 360° about any point either clockwise or counterclockwise.

A rectangle will also be carried onto itself when it is reflected over any of its lines of symmetry. A rectangle has two lines of symmetry, and a square has four.

Parallelogram

A parallelogram will be carried onto itself when it is rotated by any multiple of 180° either clockwise or counterclockwise about its center. A square or any other rhombus is carried onto itself when it is rotated about its center by a multiple of 90°. Any parallelogram will be carried onto itself when it is rotated 360° or any multiple of 360° about any point either clockwise or counterclockwise.

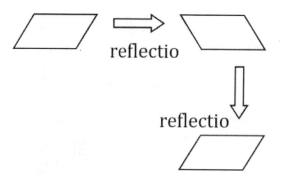

A square or other rhombus reflected across any of its four lines of symmetry will map onto itself, and a rectangle reflected across either of its two line of symmetry will be carried onto itself. Other parallelograms have no lines of symmetry and can therefore not be reflected onto themselves

<u>Trapezoid</u>

A trapezoid will be carried onto itself when it is rotated 360° or any multiple of 360° either clockwise or counterclockwise.

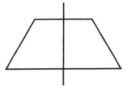

A trapezoid will be carried onto itself when it is reflected over its line of symmetry, which is the perpendicular bisector of its two parallel sides.

<u>Regular polygon</u>

A regular polygon will be carried onto itself when it is rotated about its center either clockwise or counterclockwise by $360°/n$, where n is the number of sides of the polygon.

Any polygon will be carried onto itself when it is rotated 360° or any multiple of 360° about any point either clockwise or counterclockwise.

A regular polygon will be carried onto itself when it is reflected over any of its lines of symmetry.

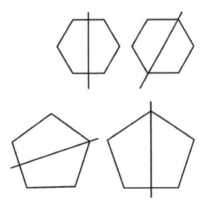

Rotation, center of rotation, and angle of rotation

A rotation is a transformation that turns a figure around a point called the center of rotation, which can lie anywhere in the plane. If a line is drawn from a point on a figure to the center of rotation, and another line is drawn from the center to the rotated image of that point, the angle between the two lines is the angle of rotation. The vertex of the angle of rotation is the center of rotation.

Reflection over a line and reflection in a point

A reflection of a figure over a line (a "flip") creates a congruent image that is the same distance from the line as the original figure but on the opposite side. The line of reflection is the perpendicular bisector of any line segment drawn from a point on the original figure to its reflected image (unless the point and its reflected image happen to be the same point, which happens when a figure is reflected over one of its own sides).

A reflection of a figure in a point is the same as the rotation of the figure 180° about that point. The image of the figure is congruent to the original figure. The point of reflection is the midpoint of a line segment which connects a point in the figure to its image (unless the point and its reflected image happen to be the same point, which happens when a figure is reflected in one of its own points).

Translation

A translation is a transformation which slides a figure from one position in the plane to another position in the plane. The original figure and the translated figure have the same size, shape, and orientation.

Rotation, reflection, and translation

To rotate a given figure: 1. Identify the point of rotation. 2. Using tracing paper, geometry software, or by approximation, recreate the figure at a new location around the point of rotation.

To reflect a given figure: 1. Identify the line of reflection. 2. By folding the paper, using geometry software, or by approximation, recreate the image at a new location on the other side of the line of reflection.

To translate a given figure: 1. Identify the new location. 2. Using graph paper, geometry software, or by approximation, recreate the figure in the new location. If using graph paper, make a chart of the x- and y-values to keep track of the coordinates of all critical points.

Dilation

Dilation is a transformation which proportionally stretches or shrinks a figure by a scale factor. The dilated image is the same shape and orientation as the original image but a different size. A polygon and its dilated image are similar.

Identifying transformation

To identify that a figure has been rotated, look for evidence that the figure is still face-up, but has changed its orientation.

To identify that a figure has been reflected across a line, look for evidence that the figure is now face-down.

To identify that a figure has been translated, look for evidence that a figure is still face-up and has not changed orientation; the only change is location.

To identify that a figure has been dilated, look for evidence that the figure has changed its size but not its orientation.

Line

A line is a straight continuous set of points and usually denoted by two points in that set. For instance, $\overleftrightarrow{AB}$ is the line which passes through points A and B.

Distance along a line and distance around a circular arc

The distance along a line, or the distance between two points on a line, can be measured using a ruler. If the two points are located on the Cartesian plane, the distance can be found using the distance formula: $d = \sqrt{(x_2 - x_1)^2 + (y_2 - y_1)^2}$.

The distance around a circular arc, or the distance along a circle between two points, can be measured using a piece of string (to follow the shape of the circle) and then a ruler. The distance can also be found by finding the portion of the circle's circumference represented by the arc.

Area and perimeter

<u>Triangles</u>

The area of a triangle is given by the formula $A = \frac{1}{2}bh$, where A is the area of the triangle, b is the length of the base, and h is the height of the triangle perpendicular to the base.

If you know the three sides of a scalene triangle, you can use the formula $A = \sqrt{s(s-a)(s-b)(s-c)}$, where A is the area, s is the semiperimeter $s = \frac{a+b+c}{2}$, and a, b, and c are the lengths of the three sides.

The perimeter of a triangle is given by the formula $P = a + b + c$, where P is the perimeter, and a, b, and c are the lengths of the three sides. In this case, the triangle may be any shape. The variables a, b, and c are not exclusive to right triangles in the perimeter formula.

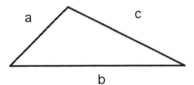

Equilateral triangle: The area of an equilateral triangle is found by the formula $A = \frac{\sqrt{3}}{4}s^2$, where A is the area and s is the length of a side. You could use the $30° - 60° - 90°$ ratios to find the height of the triangle and then use the standard triangle area formula, but this is faster.

The perimeter of an equilateral triangle is found by the formula $P = 3s$, where P is the perimeter and s is the length of a side.

If you know the length of the apothem (distance from the center of the triangle perpendicular to the base) and the length of a side, you can use the formula $A = \frac{1}{2}ap$, where a is the length of the apothem and p is the perimeter.

Isosceles triangle: The area of an isosceles triangle is found by the formula, $A = \frac{1}{2}b\sqrt{a^2 - \frac{b^2}{4}}$, where A is the area, b is the base (the unique side), and a is the length of one of the two congruent sides.

If you do not remember this formula, you can use the Pythagorean Theorem to find the height so you can use the standard formula for the area of a triangle.

The perimeter of an isosceles triangle is found by the formula

$A = 2a + b$, where P is the perimeter, a is the length of one of the congruent sides, and b is the base (the unique side).

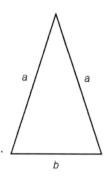

Squares

The area of a square is found by using the formula $A = s^2$, where A is the area of the square, and s is the length of one side. The perimeter of a square is found by using the formula $P = 4s$, where P is the perimeter of the square, and s is the length of one side. Because all four sides are equal in a square, it is faster to multiply the length of one side by 4 than to add the same number four times. You could use the formulas for rectangles and get the same answer.

Rectangles

The area of a rectangle is found by the formula $A = lw$, where A is the area of the rectangle, l is the length (usually considered to be the longer side) and w is the width (usually considered to be the shorter side). The numbers for l and w are interchangeable.

The perimeter of a rectangle is found by the formula $P = 2l + 2w$ or $P = 2(l + w)$, where P is the perimeter of the rectangle, l is the length, and w is the width. It may be easier to add the length and width first and then double the result, as in the second formula.

Parallelograms

The area of a parallelogram is found by the formula $A = bh$, where A is the area, b is the length of the base, and h is the height. Note that the base and height correspond to the length and width in a rectangle, so this formula would apply to rectangles as well.

The perimeter of a parallelogram is found by the formula $P = 2a + 2b$ or $P = 2(a + b)$, where P is the perimeter, and a and b are the lengths of the two sides.

Do not confuse the height of a parallelogram with the length of the second side. The two are only the same measure in the case of a rectangle.

Trapezoids

The area of a trapezoid is found by the formula $A = \frac{1}{2}h(b_1 + b_2)$, where A is the area, h is the height (segment joining and perpendicular to the parallel bases), and b_1 and b_2 are the two parallel sides (bases). Do not use one of the other two sides as the height unless that side is also perpendicular to the parallel bases.

The perimeter of a trapezoid is found by the formula $P = a + b_1 + c + b_2$, where P is the perimeter, and a, b_1, c, and b_2 are the four sides of the trapezoid. Notice that the height does not appear in this formula.

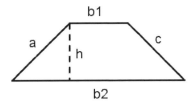

Area, circumference, and diameter of a circle

The area of a circle is found by the formula $A = \pi r^2$, where A is the area and r is the length of the radius. If the diameter of the circle is given, remember to divide it in half to get the length of the radius before proceeding.

The circumference of a circle is found by the formula $C = 2\pi r$, where C is the circumference and r is the radius. Again, remember to convert the diameter if you are given that measure rather than the radius.

To find the diameter when you are given the radius, double the length of the radius.

Lateral surface area and volume of spheres

The lateral surface area is the area around the outside of the sphere. The lateral surface area is given by the formula $A = 4\pi r^2$, where r is the radius. The answer is generally given in terms of pi. A sphere does not have separate formulas for lateral surface area and total surface area as other solid figures do. Often, a problem may ask for the surface area of a sphere. Use the above formula for all problems involving the surface area of a sphere.

The volume is given by the formula $V = \frac{4}{3}\pi r^3$, where r is the radius.

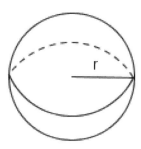

Volume and total surface area of right prisms

The volume of a right prism is found by the formula $V = Bh$, where V is the volume, B is the area of the base, and h is the height (perpendicular distance between the bases).

The total surface area is the area of the entire outside surface of a solid. The total surface area of a right prism is found by the formula $TA = 2B + $ (sum of the areas of the sides), where TA is the total surface area and B is the area of one base. To use this formula, you must remember the formulas for the planar figures.

If the problem asks for the lateral surface area (the area around the sides, not including the bases), use the formula $LA = $ sum of the areas of the sides. Again, you will need to remember the formulas for the various planar figures.

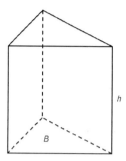

Volume and total surface area of rectangular prisms

The volume of a rectangular prism is found by the formula $V = lwh$, where V is the volume, l is the length, w is the width, and h is the height.

Total surface area is the area of the entire outside surface of the solid. The total surface area of a rectangular prism is found by the formula $TA = 2lw + 2lh + 2wh$ or $TA = 2(lw + lh + wh)$, where TA is the total surface area, l is the length, w is the width, and h is the height.

If the problem asks for lateral surface area, find the total area of the sides, but not the bases. Use the formula $LA = 2lh + 2wh$ or $LA = 2(lh + wh)$, where l is the length, w is the width, and h is the height.

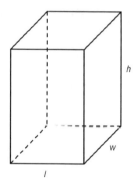

Volume and total surface area of cubes

The volume of a cube is found by the formula $V = s^3$, where V is the volume and s is the length of a side. This is the same as the formula for the volume of a rectangular prism, except the length, width, and height are all equal.

The total surface area of a cube is found by the formula $TA = 6s^2$, where TA is the total surface area and s is the length of a side. You could use the formula for the total surface area of a rectangular prism, but if you remember that all six sides of a cube are equal, this formula is much faster.

Volume, lateral surface area, and total surface area of right circular cylinders

The volume of a right circular cylinder is found by the formula $V = \pi r^2 h$, where V is the volume, r is the radius, and h is the height.

The lateral surface area is the surface area without the bases. The formula is $LA = 2\pi rh$, where LA is the lateral surface area, r is the radius, and h is the height. Remember that if you unroll a cylinder, the piece around the middle is a rectangle. The length of a side of the rectangle is equal to the circumference of the circular base, or $2\pi r$. Substitute this formula for the length, and substitute the height of the cylinder for the width in the formula for the area of a rectangle.

The total surface area of a cylinder is the lateral surface area plus the area of the two bases. The bases of a cylinder are circles, making the formula for the total surface area of a right circular cylinder $TA = 2\pi rh + 2\pi r^2$, where TA is the total area, r is the radius, and h is the height.

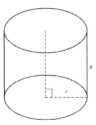

Volume of pyramids

The volume of a pyramid is found by the formula $V = \frac{1}{3}Bh$, where V is the volume, B is the area of the base, and h is the height (segment from the vertex perpendicular to the base). Notice this formula is the same as $\frac{1}{3}$ the volume of a right prism. In this formula, B represents the *area* of the base, not the length or width of the base. The base can be different shapes, so you must remember the various formulas for the areas of plane figures. In determining the height of the pyramid, use the perpendicular distance from the vertex to the base, not the slant height of one of the sides.

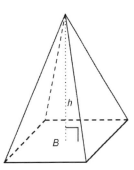

Volume, lateral surface area, and total surface area of right circular cones

The volume of a right circular cone is found by the formula $V = \frac{1}{3}\pi r^2 h$, where V is the volume, r is the radius, and h is the height. Notice this is the same as $\frac{1}{3}$ the volume of a right circular cylinder.

The lateral surface area of a right circular cone is found by the formula $LA = \pi r\sqrt{r^2 + h^2}$ or $LA = \pi rs$, where LA is the lateral surface area, r is the radius, h is the height, and s is the slant height (distance from the vertex to the edge of the circular base). $s = \sqrt{r^2 + h^2}$

- 103 -

The total surface area of a right circular cone is the same as the lateral surface area plus the area of the circular base. The formula for total surface area is $TA = \pi r\sqrt{r^2 + h^2} + \pi r^2$ or $TA = \pi rs + \pi r^2$, where TA is the total surface area, r is the radius, h is the height, and s is the slant height.

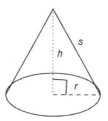

Practice Test #1

Practice Questions

1. $f(x) = 5x + 10$. If $x = 10$, then what is the value of $f(x)$?
   a. 25
   b. 60
   c. 12
   d. 5

2. The table below lists values for x and $f(x)$.

x	$f(x)$
1	2
2	5
3	10
4	17
5	26

Which of the following equations describes the relationship between x and $f(x)$?

   a. $f(x) = x + 1$
   b. $f(x) = x^2$
   c. $f(x) = (-x)^2$
   d. $f(x) = x^2 + 1$

3. Mrs. Rose has 16 students in her class. Her class has three times as many girls as boys. How many girls and boys are in Mrs. Rose's class?
   a. 12 girls, 4 boys
   b. 4 girls, 12 boys
   c. 3 girls, 1 boy
   d. 9 girls, 7 boys

Questions 4 – 8 pertain to the following bar graph:

Liz set a goal to lose 30 pounds in 12 months. The figure below contains a bar graph that describes her weight in months 1 – 12.

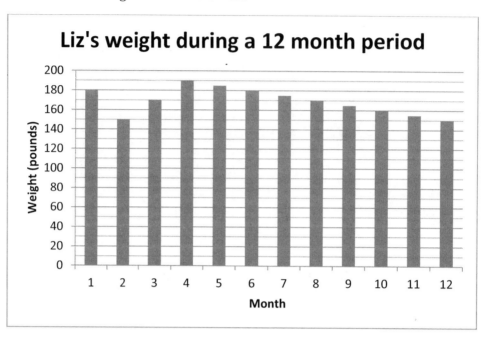

Figure: Bar graph for questions 4 – 8

4. What was Liz's initial weight?
   - a. 150 pounds
   - b. 170 pounds
   - c. 180 pounds
   - d. 195 pounds

5. How much weight did Liz lose by month 2?
   - a. 30 pounds
   - b. 20 pounds
   - c. 10 pounds
   - d. 0 pounds

6. Did Liz lose or gain weight from month 2 to month 4? How much weight did Liz lose or gain?
   - a. Liz lost 40 pounds
   - b. Liz gained 40 pounds
   - c. Liz lost 20 pounds
   - d. Liz gained 20 pounds

7. Which of the following statements is *not* supported by the weight loss data in Figure 1?
   - a. Liz lost 30 pounds by the second month of her diet.
   - b. Liz weighed more after the fourth month of her diet than she weighed at the beginning of her diet.
   - c. Liz experienced slow but consistent weight loss after month 4 of her diet.
   - d. Liz's rapid weight loss was sustainable for all 12 months of her diet.

8. Which of the following statements is most supported by the weight loss data in Figure 1?

    a. The most Liz weighed was 180 pounds over the entire course of her diet
    b. Liz lost weight every month during the entire 12 months of her diet
    c. Liz did not meet her weight loss goal
    d. Liz met her weight loss goal in month 12 through slow, consistent weight loss over time

9. Which of the following figures contains a graph of the function $y = 2x + 2$?

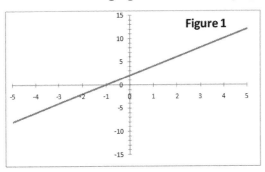
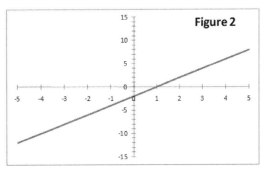
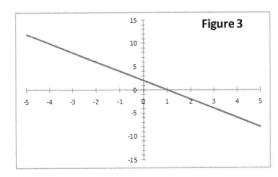
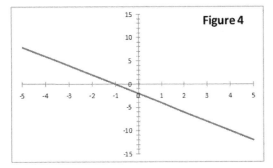

    a. Figure 1
    b. Figure 2
    c. Figure 3
    d. Figure 43

10. Which of the following figures contains a graph of the function $y = x^2 + 10$?

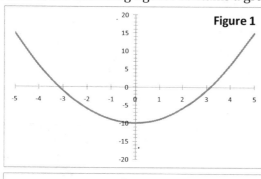

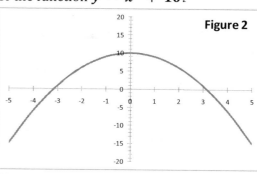

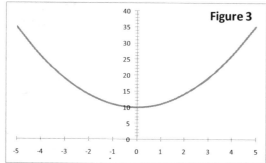

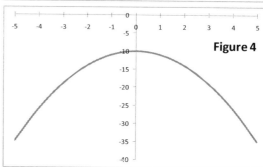

a. Figure 1
b. Figure 2
c. Figure 3
d. Figure 3

Questions 11 and 12 pertain to the following coordinate pairs:

$$\{(-5, 18), (-2, 12), (0, 3), (2,-3), (5,-12)\}$$

11. What is the domain of the coordinate pairs?
a. {18, 12, 3, -3, -12}
b. {-5, -2, 0, 2, 5}
c. {0, 3}
d. {-5, 18, 5, -12}

12. What is the range of the coordinate pairs?
a. {18, 12, 3, -3, -12}
b. {-5, -2, 0, 2, 5}
c. {0, 3}
d. {-5, 18, 5, -12}

Questions 13 and 14 pertain to the following scenario:

Aisha runs a small business selling candy bars to her classmates in school. She buys each candy bar for $0.75, and she sells each candy bar for $1.50. Let y represent Aisha's profit. Let x represent the number of candy bars she sells per day.

13. Which equation best represents Aisha's daily profit from selling candy bars?

a. $y = 0.75x - 1.50x$
b. $y = 0.75x + 0.75x$
c. $y = 1.50x + 0.75x$
d. $y = 1.50x - 0.75x$

14. Which figure contains the graph that best represents Aisha's daily profit from selling candy bars?

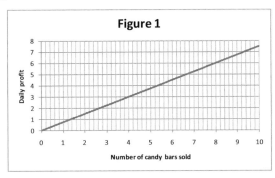

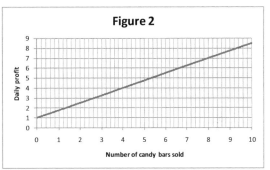

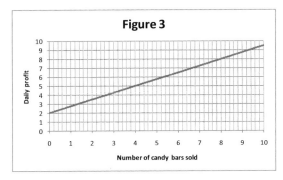

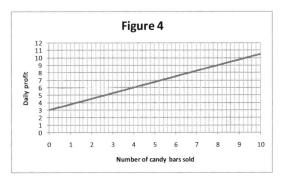

a. Figure 1
b. Figure 2
c. Figure 3
d. Figure 4

15. Consider two numbers, A and B. Let $A\Omega B = A2 + B2 - AB$. What is $2\Omega 3$?

a. 19
b. 0
c. 7
d. -1

16. What are the factors of the following polynomial: $2x^2 + 7x - 15$?

a. $(2x + 5)(x - 3)$
b. $(x + 5)(2x - 3)$
c. $(2x - 5)(x + 3)$
d. $(x - 5)(2x + 3)$

17. What is the solution to the following equation: $x^2 - 9 = 0$?
   a. $x = 3$
   b. $x = -3$
   c. Both A and B are solutions to the equation
   d. Neither A nor B is a solution to the equation

18. What is the simplest form of the following polynomial?
$$4x^3 + x - x^3 + 2x^2 + 3 - 3x^3 + x - 2x^2 - 1$$

   a. $2x + 2$
   b. $x + 1$
   c. $x^3 + 1$
   d. $2(x + 1)$

19. Which of the following equations is an example of the distributive property?
   a. $(5)(3) = (3)(5)$
   b. $5 + 3 = 3 + 5$
   c. $(5)(1 + 2) = (5)(1) + (5)(2)$
   d. $15 = 15$

20. Which of the following equations is an example of the commutative property?
   a. $(2)(7 + 8) = 14 + 16$
   b. $14 + 16 = 16 + 14$
   c. $(2)(7) + (2)(8) = (2)(15)$
   d. $30 = 30$

Questions 21 – 25 pertain to the following chart:

John noticed that the number of points he scores during a basketball game is directly related to the number of hours he spends practicing each week. The table below lists John's weekly scores as a function of hours practiced. Let *h* represent the number of hours practiced and let *p* represent the number of points scored.

Number of hours practiced	Number of points scored during basketball game
2	11
4	21
6	31
8	41
10	51

21. Can the data presented in Table 2 be represented by a linear function?
   a. Yes because the data can be written as a first-degree polynomial function of one variable.
   b. Yes because the data can be written as a second-degree polynomial function of two variables.
   c. No because the data cannot be written as a first-degree polynomial function of one variable.
   d. No because the data cannot be written as a first-degree polynomial function of two variables.

22. Which equation represents the number of points John scored as a function of the number of hours he practiced?

    a. $p(h) = 5h + 1$
    b. $p(h) = 5h - 1$
    c. $p(h) = p + 10$
    d. $p(h) = p - 10$

23. If the number of points John scored during a basketball game were written as a linear function of the number of hours he practiced, which set of numbers below would represent the domain of that function?

    a. {11, 21, 31, 41, 51}
    b. {2, 4, 6, 8, 10}
    c. {2, 11}
    d. {10, 51}

24. If the number of points John scored during a basketball game were written as a linear function of the number of hours he practiced, which set of numbers below would represent the range of that function?

    a. {11, 21, 31, 41, 51}
    b. {2, 4, 6, 8, 10}
    c. {2, 11}
    d. {10, 51}

25. Which graph below best represents the relationship between the number of hours John practiced and number of points he scored?

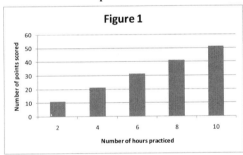

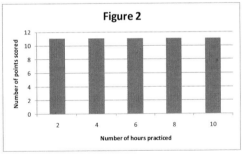

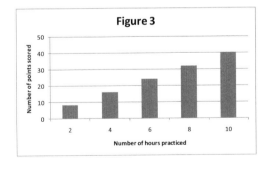

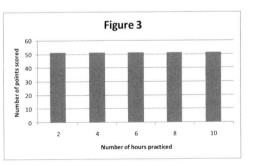

    a. Figure 1
    b. Figure 2
    c. Figure 3
    d. Figure 4

Questions 26 –28 pertain to the following graph:

The graph describes the change in distance over time for a particular car.

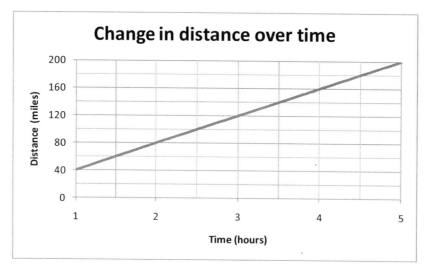

Change in distance over time

26. What is the slope of the line shown in the graph?
    a. 20
    b. 40
    c. 60
    d. 80

27. What are the units of the slope of the line?
    a. time per distance
    b. distance per time
    c. hours per miles
    d. miles per hour

28. What physical quantity does the slope measure? In other words, what does the slope tell you about the car's movement?
    a. The slope tells the car's speed
    b. The slope tells the total distance the car traveled
    c. The slope tells the total amount of time the car spent traveling
    d. The slope tells the amount of gas in the car

Questions 29 -31 pertain to the following Equation A:

Let the equation of a line be described by Equation A: $5y - 100x = 25$

29. What are the slope and y-intercept of the line?
    a. The slope is 100, and the y-intercept is 5.
    b. The slope is 5, and the y-intercept is 100.
    c. The slope is 20, and the y-intercept is 5.
    d. the slope is 25, and the y-intercept is 5.

    Suppose the equation of the same line is now described by Equation B: $5y - 200x = 75$

30. How does the slope of Equation B compare to the slope of Equation A?

    a. The slope of Equation B is half the slope of Equation A
    b. The slope of Equation B is twice the slope of Equation A
    c. The slope of Equation B is 200 times the slope of Equation A
    d. The slope of Equation B is the same as the slope of the Equation A

31. How does the y-intercept of Equation B compare to the y-intercept of Equation A?

    a. The y-intercept of Equation B is twice the y-intercept of Equation A
    b. The y-intercept of Equation B is three times the y-intercept of Equation A
    c. The y-intercept of Equation B is 75 times the y-intercept of Equation A
    d. The y-intercept of Equation B is the same as the y-intercept of Equation A

32. Line M contains the following two points: (1, 10) and (6, 20). What is the slope of line M?

    a. 5
    b. 2
    c. 0.5
    d. 10

33. Line Q has a slope of 10 and intercepts the y axis at point (0, -15). What is the equation of line Q?

    a. $y = -15$
    b. $y = -15x + 10$
    c. $y = 15x - 10$
    d. $y = 10x - 15$

34. The equation for line 1 is $y_x = 2x_1 + 6$ and the equation for line 2 is $y_2 = -x_2 - 3$. At what point does line 1 intersect line 2?

    a. (-3, 6)
    b. (6, -3)
    c. (-3, 0)
    d. (0,-3)

35. Table A below contains the x and y coordinates for several points on line P. Table B contains the x and y coordinates for several points on line Q. At what point does line P intersect line Q?

Table A: Coordinates for line P

x	y
-5	-8
-4	-4
-3	0
-2	4
-1	8
0	12
1	16

Table B: Coordinates for line Q

x	Y
-5	4
-4	2
-3	0
-2	-2
-1	-4
0	-6
1	-8

a. (-3, 0)
b. (-5, -8)
c. (0, -6)
d. (1, -8)

Questions 36 – 40 pertain to the following information:

Elli wants to plant a flower garden that contains only roses and tulips. However, she has a limited amount of space for the garden, and she can only afford to buy a specific number of each plant. Elli has enough space to plant a total of 20 flowers, and she has a total of $100 to purchase the flowers. Roses cost $14 per plant and tulips cost $4 per plant. Let R represent the number of roses and let T represent the number of tulips Elli will plant in her garden.

36. Which system of linear equations can be used to solve for the number of roses and tulips Elli will plant in her garden?

a. $\begin{cases} 4R + 14T = 20 \\ R + T = 100 \end{cases}$

b. $\begin{cases} R + T = 20 \\ 14R + 4T = 100 \end{cases}$

c. $\begin{cases} R + T = 20 \\ 4R + 14T = 100 \end{cases}$

d. $\begin{cases} 14R + 4T = 20 \\ 14R + 4T = 100 \end{cases}$

37. How many roses will Elli plant in her flower garden?

a. 4
b. 20
c. 18
d. 2

38. How many tulips will Elli plant in her flower garden?

a. 4
b. 20
c. 18
d. 2

39. Based on the information provided, why would Elli plant more tulips than roses in her garden?

a. Because tulips require less space than roses
b. Because tulips are less expensive than roses
c. Because tulips are prettier than roses
d. Because tulips require less fertilizer than roses

40. Suppose the local greenhouse has a sale, allowing Elli to purchase roses for $9 per plant. Now how many roses and tulips will Elli plant in her garden?

a. 4 roses and 16 tulips
b. 16 roses and 4 tulips
c. 9 roses and 11 tulips
d. 20 roses and 0 tulips

Questions 41 – 45 pertain to the following information:

Joshua has to earn more than 92 points on the state test in order to qualify for an academic scholarship. Each question is worth 4 points, and the test has a total of 30 questions. Let x represent the number of test questions.

41. Which of the following inequalities can be solved to determine the number of questions Joshua must answer correctly?

    a. $4x < 30$
    b. $4x < 92$
    c. $4x > 30$
    d. $4x > 92$

42. How many questions must Joshua answer correctly?

    a. $x < 30$
    b. $x < 23$
    c. $23 < x < 30$
    d. $23 < x \leq 30$

43. Which of the following graphs best represents the number of questions Joshua must answer correctly?

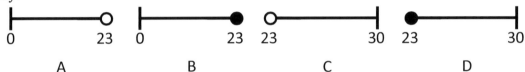

    a. Graph A
    b. Graph B
    c. Graph C
    d. Graph D

44. Let p represent the number of points. Which of the following inequalities best represents the number of points Joshua must earn on the state test?

    a. $p < 30$
    b. $p < 92$
    c. $92 < p \leq 120$
    d. $92 \leq p < 120$

45. Based on the information provided, if Joshua answers exactly 23 questions correctly, will he qualify for an academic scholarship?

    a. Yes, because he will earn exactly 92 points for answering 23 questions correctly
    b. Yes, because he will score higher than 75% for answering 23 questions correctly
    c. No, because he must answer more than 23 questions correctly
    d. No, because Joshua's parents earn too much money for him to qualify for a scholarship

Questions 46 – 49 pertain to the following information:

$$y_1 = x^2$$

$$y_2 = -x^2$$

$$y_3 = x^2 + 10$$

46. Which of the following numbers is included in the range of y_1?

    a. 0
    b. -1
    c. -2
    d. -3

47. How does function y_2 compare to the original function y_1?

    a. y_2 has a different domain than y_1.
    b. y_2 has a different range than y_1.
    c. y_2 is shifted vertically by -1 unit when compared to y_1.
    d. y_2 is shifted horizontally by -1 unit when compared to y_1.

48. How does function y_3 compare to the original function y_1?

    a. y_3 is shifted vertically by +10 units when compared to y_1
    b. y_3 is shifted vertically by -10 units when compared to y_1
    c. y_3 is shifted horizontally by +10 units when compared to y_1
    d. y_3 is shifted horizontally by -10 units when compared to y_1

49. Match the following graphs to their respective functions: y_1, y_2, and y_3.

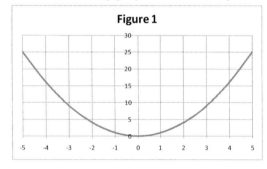

Figure 1

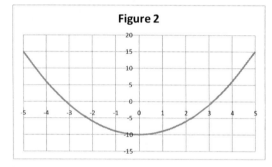

Figure 2

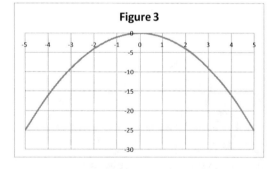

Figure 3

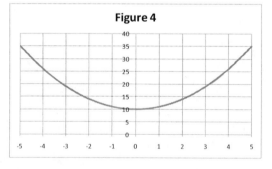

Figure 4

    a. Figure 1 contains y_1. Figure 2 contains y_2. Figure 3 contains y_3
    b. Figure 2 contains y_1. Figure 3 contains y_2. Figure 4 contains y_3
    c. Figure 1 contains y_1. Figure 3 contains y_2. Figure 4 contains y_3
    d. Figure 3 contains y_1. Figure 2 contains y_2. Figure 1 contains y_3

50. Solve the following equation for x, and write your answer in the answer grid.

$$x^2 + 10x = -25$$

-	0	0
+	1	1
	2	2
	3	3
	4	4
	5	5
	6	6
	7	7
	8	8
	9	9

51. At what value for x does the equation $x^2 + 10x = -25$ intercept the x-axis? Write your answer in the answer grid.

-	0	0
+	1	1
	2	2
	3	3
	4	4
	5	5
	6	6
	7	7
	8	8
	9	9

52. Consider the following equations:

$$x^2 = 4$$

$$x^3 = -8$$

$$x^4 = 16$$

$$x^5 = -32$$

What is x? Write your answer in the answer grid.

-	0	0
+	1	1
	2	2
	3	3
	4	4
	5	5
	6	6
	7	7
	8	8
	9	9

53. y is inversely proportional x such that $y = -\frac{1}{6}x$. If y = 5, what is x? Write your answer in the answer grid.

-	0	0
+	1	1
	2	2
	3	3
	4	4
	5	5
	6	6
	7	7
	8	8
	9	9

54. Solve the following equation for x:

$$2^x = 65536$$

Write your answer in the answer grid.

-	0	0
+	1	1
	2	2
	3	3
	4	4
	5	5
	6	6
	7	7
	8	8
	9	9

Answers and Explanations

1. B: The equation describes a functional relationship between x and $f(x)$. To solve the equation, substitute 10 as the value of x, such that $f(10) = 5(10) + 10 = 50 + 10 = 60$.

2. D: For each value of x, $f(x) = x^2 + 1$,

$$f(1) = (1)^2 + 1 = (1)(1) + 1 = 1 + 1 = 2$$
$$f(2) = (2)^2 + 1 = (2)(2) + 1 = 4 + 1 = 5$$
$$f(3) = (3)^2 + 1 = (3)(3) + 1 = 9 + 1 = 10$$
$$f(4) = (4)^2 + 1 = (4)(4) + 1 = 16 + 1 = 17$$
$$f(5) = (5)^2 + 1 = (5)(5) + 1 = 25 + 1 = 26$$

3. A: Let x represent the number of boys in Mrs. Rose's class. Since Mrs. Rose has three times as many girls in her class as boys, 3x represents the number of girls in Mrs. Rose's class. The total number of students in the class is 16. Written as an equation and solved for x we get:

$$x + 3x = 16$$
$$4x = 16$$
$$x = 4$$

Hence $x = 4$ and $3x = 12$. Therefore, 4 is the number of boys and 12 is the number of girls. Also,

$4 + 12 = 16$, the total number of students in the class.

4. C: According to the graph, in month 1, Liz weighed 180 pounds.

5. A: In month 1, Liz weighed 180 pounds. By month 2, Liz weighed 150 pounds. Since 180 – 150 = 30, Liz lost 30 pounds by month 2.

6. B: In month 2, Liz weight 150 pounds but she weighed 190 pounds in month 4. Since 190 – 150 = 40, Liz gained 40 pounds from month to month 4.

7. D: Liz experienced a rapid weight loss of 30 pounds by month 2; however she gained 40 pounds over the next 2 months, and her resulting weight was greater than her weight at the beginning of her diet. Therefore, her rapid weight loss was NOT sustainable for all 12 months of her diet.

8. D: Liz weighed 150 pounds by month 12, which was 30 pounds less than her initial 180 pounds. Thus Liz met her weight loss goal. Furthermore, from month 4 to month 12, Liz lost 5 pounds per month, which was means she met her goal through slow, consistent weight loss over time. Answer A is incorrect because Liz weight 190 pounds during month 4. Answer B is incorrect because Liz gained weight between month 2 and month 4. Answer C is incorrect because Liz did meet her 30 pound weight loss goal.

9. A: The equation is written in the form of the point slope formula: $y = mx + b$ where m is the slope of the line and b is the y-axis intercept. For the given equation $y = 2x + 2$, the slope of the line is positive 2 and the line intercepts the y-axis at positive 2. The graph in Figure 1 fits these criteria. The graph in Figure 2 intercepts the y-axis at negative 2. The graphs in Figure 3 and Figure 4 have slopes of negative 2.

10. C: The equation is written in the form $y = Ax^2 + B$ where A tells the concavity of the graph and B is the y-intercept. In this case, A equals positive 1. So the graph is concave up. B equals positive 10. So the graph intercepts the y-axis at positive 10. The graph in Figure 3 fits these criteria. The graph in Figure 1 intercepts the y-axis at negative 10. The graphs in Figure 2 and Figure 4 are concave down.

11. B: The list of coordinate pairs represents the x and y values of five points. The domain is all the x values. Answer B contains all the x values of the coordinate pairs.

12. A: The list of coordinate pairs represents the x and y values of five points. The range is all the y values. Answer A contains all the y values of the coordinate pairs.

13. D: To calculate Aisha's daily profit, first determine the amount of money Aisha earns from selling candy. Since x represents the number of candy bars she sells per day, and she sells each bar for $1.50, then her daily earnings equal 1.50x. Next, determine how much money Aisha spends buying the candy. Since each bar costs $0.75, she spends a total of 0.75x buying the candy. Finally, subtract the amount of money she spends buying the candy from the amount of money she earns selling the candy. Since y represents her daily profits,

$y = 1.50x – 0.75x$.

14. A: The graph that represents Aisha's daily profit can be determined from the equation $y = 1.50x – 0.75x$. This equation can also be written as $y = (1.50 – 0.75)x$ or $y = 0.75x$. In its simplest form, the equation that describes Aisha's profits has a y-intercept of 0 and a slope of 0.75. The y-intercept tells the profits Aisha will earn if she sells no candy bars. Based on the equation, if Aisha sells no candy bars, then she earns no profit. The graph in Figure 1 fits these criteria.

15. C: Based on the definition of $A\Omega B$,

$$2\,\Omega 3 = 2^2 + 3^2 - (2)(3)$$

$$= 4 + 9 - 6$$

$$= 13 - 6$$

$$= 7$$

16. B: To factor the polynomial, find factors of the first and third term whose product can be added to get the middle term. The fastest way to find the correct answer is to multiply the answer choices and select the choice that yields the original equation. In this case,

$$(x + 5)(2x - 3) = (x)(2x) + (x)(-3) + (5)(2x) + (5)(-3)$$

$$= 2x^2 - 3x + 10x - 15$$

$$= 2x^2 + 7x - 15$$

17. C: The solution to the equation follows:

$$x^2 - 9 = 0$$

$$x^2 = 9$$

$$x = \sqrt{9}$$

$$x = +3 \ and \ x = -3$$

18. D: To simplify the polynomial, group and combine all terms of the same order.

$$4x^3 + x - x^3 + 2x^2 + 3 - 3x^3 + x - 2x^2 - 1$$
$$= (4x^3 - x^3 - 3x^3) + (2x^2 - 2x^2) + (x + x) + (3 - 1)$$
$$= 0 + 0 + 2x + 2$$
$$= 2(x + 1)$$

19. C: The distributive property says that terms inside a set of parentheses can be multiplied by a factor outside the parentheses. In other words, $a(b + c) = ab + ac$. Answer C fits this definition.

20. B: A mathematical operation is commutative if altering the order does not alter the result of the operation. In other words, $a + b = b + a$ or $ab = ba$. Answer B fits this definition.

21. A: By definition, a linear function is a first degree polynomial function of one variable, and the data shown in Table 2 can be written as such. The variable is the number of hours practiced, and the score is a function of that variable.

22. A: In each case, the number of points scored p equals 5(h) + 1 where h is the number of hours practiced. For example, $11 = (5)(2) + 1$ and $21 = (5)(4) + 1$. For answers C and D, the points scored are not written as functions of the hours practiced.

23. B: The domain consists of all the values of the independent variable. In this case, the independent variable is the number of hours practiced.

24. A: The range consists of all the values of the dependent variable. In this case, the depended variable is the number of points scored.

25. A: The bar graph shown in Figure 1 is the only graph where the number of points scored corresponds to the number of hours practiced as presented in Table 2.

26. B: The slope of a line describes the change in the dependent variable divided by the change in the independent variable, i.e. the change in y over the change in x. To calculate the slope, consider any two points on the line. Let the first point be $(1, 40)$, and let the second point be $(2, 80)$.

$$\frac{y_2 - y_1}{x_2 - x_1} = \frac{80 - 40}{2 - 1} = \frac{40}{1} = 40$$

27. D: The slope of the line is the change in y divided by the change in x. Therefore, the units of the slope are the units of y over the units for x. The unit for y is the unit for distance or miles. The unit for x is the unit for time or hours. Hence the units of the slope are miles over hour or miles per hour.

28. A: The slope describes the change in distance over the change in time. The change in distance over the change in time is a measure of the car's speed in miles per hour.

29. C: First write Equation A in slope-intercept form: $y = mx + b$ where m is the slope and b is the y-intercept.

$$5y - 100x = 25$$

$$5y = 100x + 25$$

$$y = 20x + 5$$

Based on the slope-intercept form of Equation A, the slope, m = 20 and the y-intercept, b = 5.

30. B: Write Equation B in slope-intercept form, which is $y = mx + b$:

$$5y - 200x = 75$$

$$5y = 200x + 75$$

$$y = 40x + 15$$

Based on the slope-intercept form of Equation B, the slope is 40, which is twice the slope of Equation A.

31. B: Based on the slope-intercept form of Equation B which is $y = mx + b$, the y-intercept is 15, which is three time the y-intercept of Equation A.

32. B: The slope of a line is the change in y divided by the change in x. Calculate the slope as follows:

$$m = \frac{y_2 - y_1}{x_2 - x_1} = \frac{20 - 10}{6 - 1} = \frac{10}{5} = 2$$

33. D: Write the equation in slope-intercept form: $y = mx + b$ where m is the slope of the line and b is the y-intercept. In this case, the slope m = 10 and the y-intercept b = -15. Hence $y = 10x - 15$.

34. C: At the intersection point of line 1 and line 2, $y_1 = y_2 = y$ and $x_1 = x_2 = x$. To find the x coordinate, let $y_1 = y_2$.

$$2x + 6 = -x - 3$$

$$2x + x = -6 - 3$$

$$3x = -9$$

$$x = -3$$

Now find the y coordinate by substituting x = -3 into either the equation for line 1 or the equation for line2.

$$y = 2x + 6$$

$$y = (2)(-3) + 6$$

$$y = -6 + 6$$

$$y = 0$$

Therefore, the point of intersection is (-3, 0).

35. A: The intersection point of line P and line Q will be common to both lines. See the explanation for question 34. Point (-3, 0) is the only point that is common to both lines.

36. B: Since Elli will plant a total of 20 flowers, the number of roses plus the number of tulips is 20 or $R + T = 20$. Each rose costs $14; so multiply the number of roses by 14. Each tulip costs $4; so multiply the number of tulips by 4. Elli has a total of $100 to spend on roses and tulips. So $14R + 4T = 100$.

37. D: Use a linear system of equations to find the number of roses. See the explanation for question 36. In this case, the system of equations is $R + T = 20$ and $14R + 4T = 100$. Begin with $R + T = 20$ and solve for T.

$$R + T = 20$$

$$T = 20 - R$$

Now substitute the equation for T into the equation $14R + 4T = 100$.

$$14R + 4T = 100$$

$$14R + 4(20 - R) = 100$$

$$14R + 80 - 4R = 100$$

$$10R = 20$$

$$R = 2$$

Therefore, Elli will plant 2 roses in her garden.

38. C: The number of roses, R is 2 and $R + T = 20$. Therefore, $T = 20 - 2 = 18$. Hence, Elli will plant 18 tulips in her garden.

39. B: Based on the given information, roses cost $14 while tulips cost only $4. Therefore, tulips are less expensive than roses. No information is given about the amount of space or fertilizer tulips require or about which flower Elli thinks is prettier.

40. A: The new price for roses requires defining a new system of equations. Elli will still plant a total of 20 flowers. Hence

$$R + T = 20$$

$$T = 20 - R$$

However, based on the new price for roses,

$$9R + 4T = 100$$

$$9R + 4(20 - R) = 100$$

$$9R + 80 - 4R = 100$$

$$5R = 20$$

$$R = 4$$

At the new price for roses, Elli will plant 4 roses in her garden. Since $R + T = 20$, Elli will plant 16 tulips in her garden.

41. D: In order to determine the number of questions Joshua must answer correctly, consider the number of points he must earn. Joshua will receive 4 points for each question he answers correctly, and x represents the number of questions. Therefore, Joshua will receive a total of 4x points for all the questions he answers correctly. Joshua must earn more than 92 points. Therefore, to determine the number of questions he must answer correctly, solve the inequality $4x > 92$.

42. D: See the explanation for question 41. To determine the number of questions Joshua must correctly answer, solve the following inequality:

$$4x > 92$$

$$x > \frac{92}{4}$$

$$x > 23$$

Therefore, Joshua must correctly answer at more than 23 questions to qualify for the scholarship. Because the test has a total of 30 questions, Joshua could answer all 30 questions correctly. Hence, the best inequality to describe the number of questions Joshua must correctly answer is $23 < x \leq 30$.

43. C: The inequality that best represents the number of questions Joshua must answer correctly is $23 < x \leq 30$. Hence, the left endpoint of the graph is 23, and the right endpoint is 30. Because Joshua must answer more than 23 questions, the endpoint at 23 is not included in the data set and is represented by an open circle.

44. C: According to the statement of the problem, Joshua must earn more than 92 points. Therefore, answers A and B are incorrect. Furthermore, answer D is incorrect because this answer says his score can equal 92 points but Joshua needs more than 92 points. Because the test has a total of 30 questions, and each question is worth 4 points, Joshua can earn a maximum of $(4)(30)$ or 120 points. Hence the best inequality is $92 < p \leq 120$.

45. C: Answers A and B are incorrect because Joshua must earn more than 92 points, which means he must correctly answer more than 23 questions. Answer D is incorrect because the problem statement mentions nothing about parental earnings.

46. A: The range is all the y values. Refer to a graph of y_1 shown below.

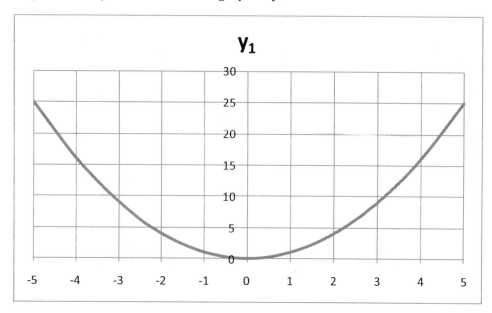

The minimum value for y is 0. Another way to solve this problem is to substitute the potential y values in the equation for y_1. For example,

$$y_1 = x^2$$
$$-1 = x^2$$
$$\sqrt{-1} = x$$

This statement has no real solution since it requires taking the square root of a negative number. Similar solutions are obtained if y = -2 or if y = -3.

47. B: The original function y_1 is concave up. See the graph of y_1 shown in the explanation for problem 46. Changing the coefficient of x^2 from +1 to -1 causes the function to be concave down. See the graph of y_2 shown below.

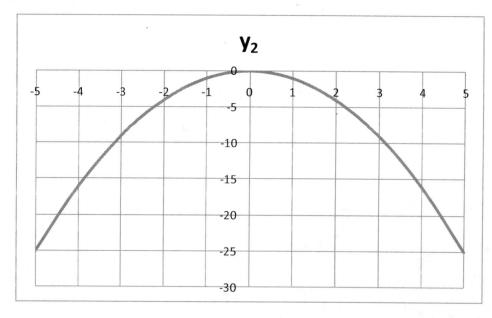

- 126 -

The y values for y_2 are different from those of y_1. Therefore, y_2 has a different range than y_1.

48. A: For function y_1, the y-intercept is 0. See the graph of y_1 shown in the explanation for <u>problem 46</u>. For function y_3, the y-intercept is +10. See the graph of y_3 shown below.

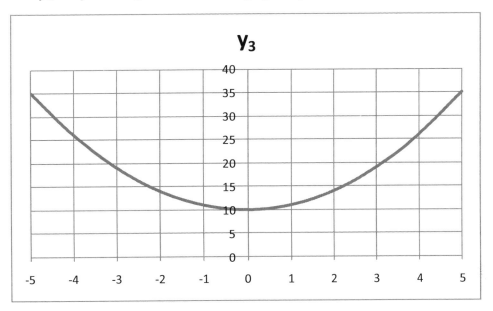

The graph of y_3 is similar to that of y_1 except the y-intercept of y_3 is 10 units above that of y_1. In other words, the difference between +10 and 0 is 10 units.

49. C: The graphs for y_1, y_2, and y_3 are displayed in the explanations for questions 46 – 48.

50. The correct answer is **x = -5**. The solution follows:

$$x^2 + 10x = -25$$

$$x^2 + 10x + 25 = 0$$

$$(x + 5)(x + 5) = 0$$

$$x = -5$$

51. The correct answer is **x = -5**. The x-intercept is determined by setting the equation equal to zero and then solving for x. When $x^2 + 10x + 25 = 0$, then x = -5.

52. The correct answer is **x = -2**. Because $x^2 = 4$, we can quickly determine that the magnitude of x is 2. The sign, however, alternates between positive and negative. Therefore, x must be -2. Note that multiplying a negative number by itself an even number of times yields a positive number. Multiplying a negative number by itself an odd number of times yields a negative number.

53. The correct answer is **x = -30**. The solution follows:

$$y = -\frac{1}{6}x$$
$$6y = -x$$
$$-6y = x$$
$$(-6)(5) = x$$
$$-30 = x$$

- 127 -

54. The correct answer is **x = 16**. The solution follows:

$$2^x = 65536$$
$$x\log 2 = \log 65536$$
$$x = \frac{\log 65536}{\log 2}$$
$$x = 16$$

Practice Test #2

Practice Questions

1. $p(y) = \frac{4y}{2} + 5$. If $y = 4$, then what is the value of $p(y)$?

    a. 9
    b. 7
    c. 13
    d. 37

2. The table below lists values for y and p(y).

y	p(y)
1	2
-1	2
2	5
-2	5
3	10
-3	10

Which of the following equations describes the relationship between y and p(y)?

    a. $p(y) = y + 1$
    b. $p(y) = 2y + 1$
    c. $p(y) = (y)^2$
    d. $p(y) = (y)^2 + 1$

3. Mr. Robinson has 20 students in his martial arts class. The ratio of boys to girls is 4:1. How many boys and girls are in Mr. Robinson's class?

    a. 15 boys, 5 girls
    b. 5 boys, 15 girls
    c. 16 boys, 4 girls
    d. 4 boys, 16 girls

Questions 4 – 6 pertain to the following passage:

> Mrs. Langston owns an orchard with several different kinds of fruit trees. Half the trees are apple trees, one quarter are pear trees, approximately one eighth are orange trees and about one eighth are lemon trees.

4. Which of the pie graphs below best describes the percentage of trees in Mrs. Langston's orchard?

    a. Figure A
    b. Figure B
    c. Figure C
    d. Figure D

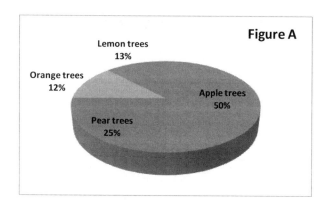

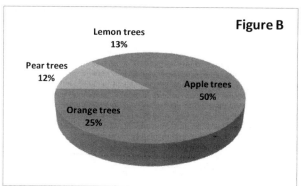

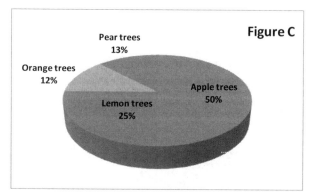

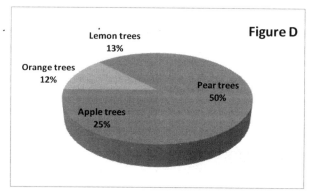

5. If Mrs. Langston has a total of 100 trees in her orchard, how many of each type of tree does she have?

    a. 50 apple trees, 25 orange trees, 13 lemon trees, and 12 pear trees
    b. 50 apple trees, 25 pear trees, 13 lemon trees, and 12 orange trees
    c. 50 apple trees, 25 lemon trees, 13 pear trees, and 12 orange trees
    d. 50 pear trees, 25 apple trees, 13 lemon trees, and 12 orange trees

6. Let y= the number of apple trees and let p(y) = the number of pear trees in Mrs. Langston's orchard. Which of the following equations best represents the relationship between apple trees and pear trees?

    a. $p(y) = 2y$
    b. $p(y) = \frac{y}{2}$
    c. $p(y) = \frac{y}{4}$
    d. $p(y) = \frac{y}{8}$

7. Based on the ratio of trees in Mrs. Langston's, she could probably produce the largest amount of which of the following products?

    a. Lemonade
    b. Orange juice
    c. Apple sauce
    d. Pear preserves

8. Based on the ratio of trees Mrs. Langston has in her orchard, which of the following statements is most likely false?

    a. Mrs. Langston plants fewer lemon trees and orange trees because she earns the least amount of money from selling these fruits.
    b. Mrs. Langston plants fewer pear trees than apple trees because pears are less profitable than apples.
    c. Mrs. Langston plants more apple trees than any other kind of fruit because she earns the most money from selling apples.
    d. Mrs. Langston plants more pear trees than any other kind of fruit because she earns the most money from selling pears.

9. Which of the following figures contains a graph of the function y = -3x – 3?

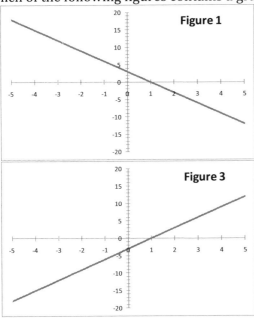
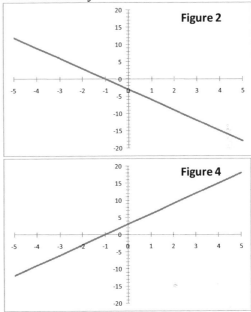

    a. Figure 1
    b. Figure 2
    c. Figure 3
    d. Figure 4

10. Which of the following figures contains a graph of the function $y = -x^2 - 5$?

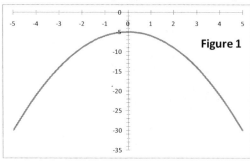

Figure 1

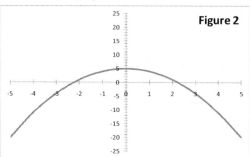

Figure 2

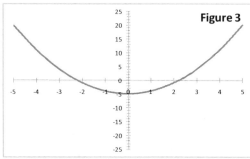

Figure 3

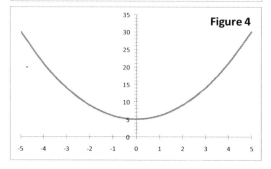

Figure 4

   a. Figure 1
   b. Figure 2
   c. Figure 3
   d. Figure 4

Questions 11 – 12 pertain to the following coordinate pairs:

    {(5,8), (3,4), (-1,-4), (-3, -8), (-5,-12)}

11. What is the range of the coordinate pairs?
   a. {5, 8, -5, -12}
   b. {-1, -4}
   c. {-5, -3, -1, 3, 5}
   d. {-12, -8, -4, 4, 8}

12. What is the domain of the coordinate pairs?
   a. {5, 8, -5, -12}
   b. {-1, -4}
   c. {-5, -3, -1, 3, 5}
   d. {-12, -8, -4, 4, 8}

Questions 13 – 14 pertain to the following scenario:

During the summers, Tyrone earns money by mowing lawns in his neighborhood. For each lawn he mows, Tyrone charges $10 per hour plus a $10 fee to cover gas and maintenance for his lawn mower. Let y represent the money Tyrone earns from mowing a single lawn. Let x represent the number of hours Tyrone spends mowing a single lawn.

13. Which equation best represents the amount of money Tyrone earns from mowing a single lawn?

    a. y = 20x
    b. y = 10x
    c. y = 10x + 10
    d. y = 10x – 10

14. Which figure contains the graph that best represents Tyrone's earnings per lawn?

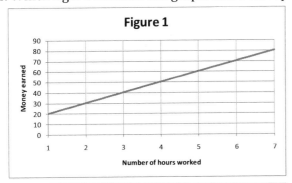
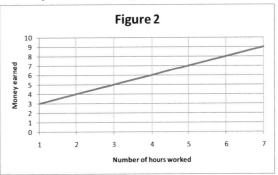
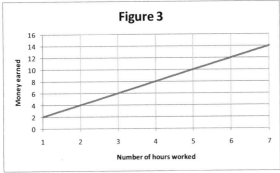
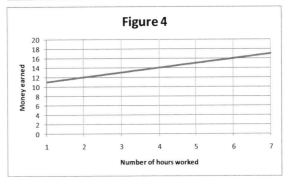

    a. Figure 1
    b. Figure 2
    c. Figure 3
    d. Figure 4

15. Consider two numbers, A and B. Let $A\theta B = 2A + 3B - A - B$. What is $1\theta 2$?

    a. 4
    b. 5
    c. 0
    d. 8

16. What are the factors of the following polynomial: $x^2 - x - 56$?

    a. $(x - 7)(x + 8)$
    b. $(x + 7)(x - 8)$
    c. $(x - 7)(x - 8)$
    d. $(x + 7)(x + 8)$

17. What is the solution to the following equation: $x^2 - 25 = 0$?

    a. x = 5
    b. x = -5
    c. Neither A nor B is a solution to the equation
    d. Both A and B are solutions to the equation

18. What is the simplest form of the following polynomial:

$$4x^3 + 5x - x^3 + 2x^2 + 17 - 3x^3 + 5x - 2x^2 + 3$$

    a. 10x + 20
    b. X + 2
    c. 10 (x + 2)
    d. $4x^3 + 2$

19. Which of the following equations is an example of the commutative property?

    a. $(3)(6 + 10) = 18 + 30$
    b. $18 + 30 = 30 + 18$
    c. $(3)(6) + (3)(10) = 3(16)$
    d. $48 = 48$

20. Which of the following equations is an example of the distributive property?

    a. $(4)(2) = (2)(4)$
    b. $4 + 2 = 2 + 4$
    c. $(2)(1 + 3) = (2)(1) + (2)(3)$
    d. $8 = 8$

Gwendolyn noticed that the number of points she scores during a basketball game is directly related to the number of hours she spends practicing each week. The table below lists Gwendolyn's weekly scores as a function of hours practiced. Let h represent the number of hours practiced and let p represent the number of points scored.

Number of hours practiced	Number of points scored during basketball game
2	8
4	14
6	20
8	26
10	32

21. Can the data presented in Table 2 be represented by a linear function?

    a. Yes because the data can be written as a second-degree polynomial function of two variables.
    b. Yes because the data can be written as a first-degree polynomial function of one variable.
    c. No because the data cannot be written as a first-degree polynomial function of one variable.
    d. No because the data cannot be written as a first-degree polynomial function of two variables.

22. Which equation represents the number of points Gwendolyn scored as a function of the number of hours she practiced?

    a. $p(h) = 3h + 2$
    b. $p(h) = 3h - 2$
    c. $p(h) = p + 6$
    d. $p(h) = p - 6$

23. If the number of points Gwendolyn scored during a basketball game were written as a linear function of the number of hours she practiced, which set of numbers below would represent the range of that function?

    a. $\{10, 32\}$
    b. $\{2, 8\}$
    c. $\{2, 4, 6, 8, 10\}$
    d. $\{8, 14, 20, 26, 32\}$

24. If the number of points Gwendolyn scored during a basketball game were written as a linear function of the number of hours she practiced, which set of numbers below would represent the domain of that function?

    a. $\{10, 32\}$
    b. $\{2, 8\}$
    c. $\{2, 4, 6, 8, 10\}$
    d. $\{8, 14, 20, 26, 32\}$

25. Which graph below best represents the relationship between the number of hours Gwendolyn practiced and number of points she scored?

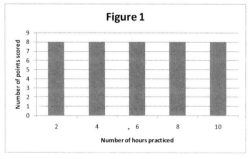

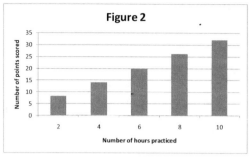

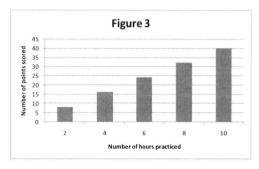

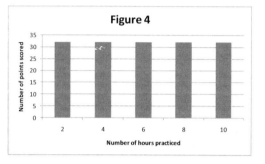

a. Figure 1
b. Figure 2
c. Figure 3
d. Figure 4

The following graph describes the change in distance over time for a cheetah hunting her prey. Use this graph to answer question 26 – question 28:

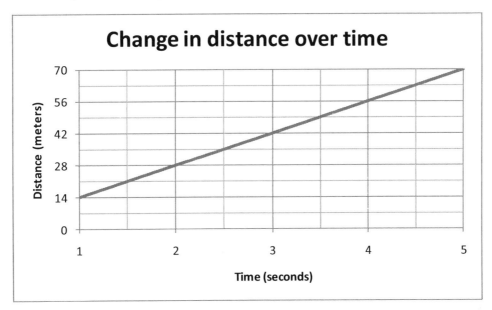

26. What is the slope of the line shown in the graph?

    a. 28
    b. 21
    c. 14
    d. 7

27. What are the units of the slope of the line?

    a. seconds per meter
    b. time per distance
    c. meters per second
    d. distance per time

28. What physical quantity does the slope measure? In other words, what does the slope tell you about the cheetah's movement?

    a. The slope tells the cheetah's speed
    b. The slope tells the total distance the cheetah traveled
    c. The slope tells the total amount of time the cheetah spent chasing her prey
    d. The slope tells how long the cheetah sleeps

Use Equation A to answer question 29 – question 31:

Let the equation of a line be described by Equation A:

$$10y - 5x = 40.$$

29. What are the y-intercept and slope of the line?

    a. The y-intercept is 40, and the slope is 10
    b. The y-intercept is 10, and the slope is 40
    c. The y-intercept is 40, and the slope is 2
    d. The y-intercept is 4, and the slope is 0.5

30. Suppose the equation of the same line is now described by Equation B:
$$10y - 10x = 20.$$

How does the slope of Equation B compare to the slope of Equation A?

   a. The slope of Equation B is twice the slope of Equation A.
   b. The slope of Equation B is the same as the slope of Equation A.
   c. The slope of Equation B is half the slope of Equation A.
   d. The slope of Equation B cannot be determined.

31. How does the y-intercept of Equation B compare to the y-intercept of Equation A?

   a. The y-intercept of Equation B is twice the y-intercept of Equation A
   b. The y-intercept of Equation B is the same as the y-intercept of Equation A
   c. The y-intercept of Equation B is half the y-intercept of Equation A
   d. The y-intercept of Equation B cannot be determined

32. Line W contains the following two points: (3, 30) and (8, 75). What is the slope of line W?
   a. 3
   b. 9
   c. 30
   d. 75

33. Line G has a slope of 20 and intercepts the y axis at point (0, 100). What is the equation of line G?

   a. $y = 100$
   b. $y = 20$
   c. $y = 20x - 100$
   d. $y = 20x + 100$

34. The equation for line 1 is $y_1 = 8x_1 - 16$ and the equation for line 2 is $y_2 = -4x_2 + 20$. At what point does line 1 intersect line 2?
   a. (3, 8)
   b. (8, 3)
   c. (-16, 20)
   d. (20, -16)

35. Table A below contains the x and y coordinates for several points on line P. Table B contains the x and y coordinates for several points on line Q. At what point does line P intersect line Q?

Table A: Coordinates for line P

x	y
5	56
1	24
-3	-8
-9	-56
-20	-144

Table B: Coordinates for line Q

x	Y

5	0
1	-16
-3	-32
-9	-56
-20	-100

a. (-20, -100)
b. (-9, -56)
c. (1, 24)
d. (5, 56)

Questions 36 – 40 pertain to the following information:

Vivian wants to plant a vegetable garden that contains only tomatoes and cucumbers. However, she has a limited amount of space for the garden, and she can only afford to buy a specific number of each vegetable. Vivian has enough space to plant a total of 40 vegetables, and she has a total of $80 to purchase the vegetables. Tomatoes cost $1 per plant and cucumbers cost $3 per plant. Let T represent the number of tomatoes and let C represent the number of cucumbers Vivian will plant in her garden.

36. Which system of linear equations can be used to solve for the number of tomatoes and cucumbers Vivian will plant in her garden?
   a. $T + C = 40$ and $T + 3C = 80$
   b. $T + 3C = 40$ and $T + C = 80$
   c. $T + C = 80$ and $T + 3C = 40$
   d. $3T + C = 80$ and $T + C = 40$

37. How many tomatoes will Vivian plant in her vegetable garden?
   a. 10
   b. 20
   c. 30
   d. 40

38. How many cucumbers will Vivian plant in her vegetable garden?
   a. 10
   b. 20
   c. 30
   d. 40

39. Based on the information provided, is it possible that Vivian will plant the same number of tomatoes as cucumbers?
   a. No, because cucumbers cost 3 times as much as tomatoes
   b. No, because cucumbers require more space than tomatoes
   c. Yes, because Vivian has enough money to purchase the same amount of tomatoes and cucumbers, despite the price difference
   d. Yes, because Vivian likes tomatoes and cucumbers equally

40. Suppose Vivian landscapes her yard, and now she has enough space to plant a total of 50 vegetables. How many tomatoes and cucumbers will Vivian plant in her garden?

    a. 25 tomatoes and 25 cucumbers
    b. 40 tomatoes and 10 cucumbers
    c. 15 tomatoes and 35 cucumbers
    d. 35 tomatoes and 15 cucumbers

Questions 41 – 45 pertain to the following information:

    Matthew has to earn more than 96 points on his high school entrance exam in order to be eligible for varsity sports. Each question is worth 3 points, and the test has a total of 40 questions. Let x represent the number of test questions.

41. Which of the following inequalities can be solved to determine the number of questions Matthew must answer correctly?

    a. $3x > 96$
    b. $3x < 96$
    c. $3x > 40$
    d. $3x < 40$

42. How many questions can Matthew answer incorrectly and still qualify for varsity sports?

    a. $x > 32$
    b. $x > 8$
    c. $0 \leq x < 8$
    d. $0 < x \leq 8$

43. Which of the following graphs best represents the number of questions Matthew can answer incorrectly?

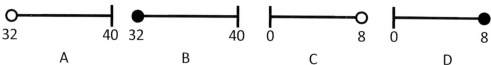

    a. Graph A
    b. Graph B
    c. Graph C
    d. Graph D

44. Let p represent the number of points. Which of the following inequalities best represents the number of points Matthew must earn on the entrance exam?

    a. $96 \leq p < 120$
    b. $96 < p \leq 120$
    c. $p < 96$
    d. $p < 32$

45. Based on the information provided, if Matthew answers exactly 32 questions correctly, will he qualify for varsity sports?

    a. Yes, because he will earn exactly 96 points for answering 32 questions correctly
    b. Yes, because he will score 80% for answering 32 questions correctly
    c. No, because he must answer more than 32 questions correctly
    d. No, because Matthew would rather get a part-time job than play varsity sports

Questions 46 – 49 pertain to the following information:

$$y_1 = 2x^2 + 3$$

$$y_2 = -2x^2 + 3$$

$$y_3 = 2x^2 - 3$$

46. Which of the following numbers is included in the range of y_1?

    a. 0
    b. 1
    c. 2
    d. 3

47. How does function y_2 compare to the original function y_1?

    a. y_2 has a different domain than y_1
    b. y_2 has a different range than y_1
    c. y_2 is shifted vertically by -2 units when compared to y_1
    d. y_2 is shifted horizontally by -2 units when compared to y_1

48. How does function y_3 compare to the original function y_1?

    a. y_3 is shifted vertically by -3 units when compared to y_1
    b. y_3 is shifted vertically by -6 units when compared to y_1
    c. y_3 is shifted vertically by +3 units when compared to y_1
    d. y_3 is shifted vertically by +6 units when compared to y_1

49. Match the following graphs to their respective functions: y_1, y_2, and y_3.

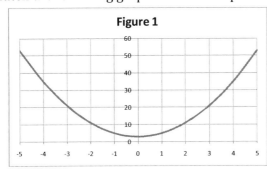

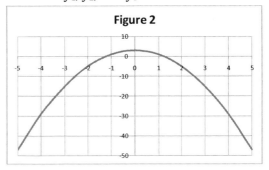

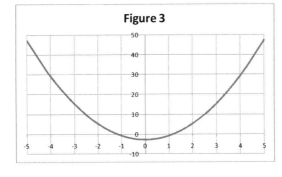

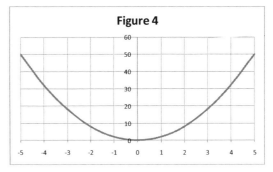

    a. Figure 1 contains y_1. Figure 2 contains y_2. Figure 3 contains y_3
    b. Figure 2 contains y_1. Figure 3 contains y_2. Figure 4 contains y_3
    c. Figure 4 contains y_1. Figure 3 contains y_2. Figure 2 contains y_3
    d. Figure 3 contains y_1. Figure 2 contains y_2. Figure 1 contains y_3

50. Solve the following equation for x, and write your answer in the answer grid.

$$x^2 + 4x = -4$$

-	0	0
+	1	1
	2	2
	3	3
	4	4
	5	5
	6	6
	7	7
	8	8
	9	9

51. At what value for x does the equation $x^2 + 4x = -4$ intercept the x-axis? Write your answer in the answer grid.

-	0	0
+	1	1
	2	2
	3	3
	4	4
	5	5
	6	6
	7	7
	8	8
	9	9

52. Consider the following equations:

$$x^2 = 1 \qquad x^3 = -1 \qquad x^4 = 1 \qquad x^5 = -1$$

What is x? Write your answer in the answer grid.

-	0	0
+	1	1
	2	2
	3	3
	4	4
	5	5
	6	6
	7	7
	8	8
	9	9

53. y is inversely proportional to x such that $y = -\frac{1}{3}x$. If y = 9, what is x? Write your answer in the answer grid.

-	0	0
+	1	1
	2	2
	3	3
	4	4
	5	5
	6	6
	7	7
	8	8
	9	9

54. Solve the following equation for x:

$$2^x = 4096$$

Write your answer in the answer grid.

-	0	0
+	1	1
	2	2
	3	3
	4	4
	5	5
	6	6
	7	7
	8	8
	9	9

Answers and Explanations

1. C: The equation describes a functional relationship between y and p(y). To solve the equation, substitute 4 as the value of y, such that

$$p(4) = \frac{4(4)}{2} + 5 = \frac{16}{2} + 5 = 8 + 5 = 13.$$

2. D: For each value of y, $p(y) = (y)^2 + 1$

$$p(1) = (1)^2 + 1 = (1)(1) + 1 = 1 + 1 = 2$$
$$p(-1) = (-1)^2 + 1 = (-1)(-1) + 1 = 1 + 1 = 2$$
$$p(2) = (2)^2 + 1 = (2)(2) + 1 = 4 + 1 = 5$$
$$p(-2) = (-2)^2 + 1 = (-2)(-2) + 1 = 4 + 1 = 5$$
$$p(3) = (3)^2 + 1 = (3)(3) + 1 = 9 + 1 = 10$$
$$p(-3) = (-3)^2 + 1 = (-3)(-3) + 1 = 9 + 1 = 10$$

3. C: Let y = the number of girls in Mr. Robinson's class. The ratio of boys to girls is 4:1. So for every 1 girl in the class, there are 4 boys in the class. Therefore, 4y equals the number of boys in Mr. Robinson's class. The total number of students in the class is 20. Therefore, the number of boys plus the number of girls equals 20 or

$$y + 4y = 20$$

$$5y = 20$$

$$y = 4$$

Hence y = 4 and 4y = 16. Therefore, 4 = the number of girls and 16 = the number of boys. Also, 4 + 16 = 20, the total number of students in the class.

4. A: Since half of the orchard contains apple trees, apple trees = 50%. In other words, $\frac{1}{2} = 0.5 = 50\%$. One quarter of the orchard contains pear trees. So pear trees = 25% or $\frac{1}{4} = 0.25 = 25\%$. Approximately one eighth of the orchard contains orange trees and one eighth contains lemon trees. One eighth is 12.5%, rounded to nearest whole number gives orange trees = 12% and lemon trees = 13%.

5. B: We know that apple trees = 50%, pear trees = 25%, lemon trees = 13%, and orange trees = 12%. Each percentage represents a portion of the total 100%. If the total number of trees is 100, then

apple trees = (50%) (100) = (0.5)(100) = 50 trees,
pear trees = (25%)(100) = (0.25)(100) = 25 trees,
lemon trees = (13%)(100) = (0.13)(100) = 13 trees,
orange trees = (12%)(100) = (0.12)(100) = 12 trees

6. B: Let y represent the number of apple trees. Then $p(y)$ represents the number of pear trees as a function of apple trees. Since Mrs. Langston has half as many pear trees as apple trees, the relationship can be represented as $(y) = \frac{1}{2}y = \frac{y}{2}$.

7. C: Mrs. Langston has more apples in her orchard than any other fruit. Therefore, she could most likely produce the largest amount of a product that comes from apples, which in this case, is apple sauce.

8. D: The statement is false because Mrs. Langston did not plant more pear trees than any other kind of fruit. Instead, she planted the most *apple* trees.

9. B: The equation is written in the form of the point slope formula:

$y = mx + b$ where m is the slope of the line and b is the y-axis intercept. For the given equation, $y = -3x - 3$, the slope of the line is negative 3 and the line intercepts the y-axis at negative 3. The graph in Figure 2 fits these criteria. The graph in Figure 1 intercepts the y-axis at positive 3. The graphs in Figure 3 and Figure 4 have slopes of positive 3.

10. A: The equation is written in the form $y = Ax^2 + B$ where A tells the concavity of the graph and B is the y- intercept. In this case, A equals negative 1. So the graph is concave down. B equals negative 5. So the graph intercepts the y-axis at negative 5. The graph in Figure 1 fits these criteria. The graph in Figure 2 intercepts the y-axis at positive 5. The graphs in Figure 3 and Figure 4 are concave up.

11. D: The list of coordinate pairs represents the x and y values of five points. The range is all the y values. Answer D contains all the y values of the coordinate pairs.

12. C: The list of coordinate pairs represents the x and y values of five points. The domain is all the x values. Answer C contains all the x values of the coordinate pairs.

13. C: Tyrone earns $10 per hour, and he works x number of hours. Therefore, he earns 10x for his time spent mowing a lawn. Furthermore, Tyrone charges an additional $10 for each lawn he mows. Therefore, his total earnings per lawn are calculated by: $y = 10x + 10$.

14. A: The graph that represents Tyrone's earnings per lawn can be determined from the equation $y = 10x + 10$, since Tyrone earns $10 for every x hours he spends mowing, with an additional overhead of $10 per job. This equation has a slope of 10. Furthermore, if Tyrone spends just 1 hour mowing a lawn, then he earns $20. The graph in Figure 1 fits these criteria.

15. B: Based on the definition of $A\theta B$,

$$
\begin{aligned}
1\theta 2 &= (2)(1) + (3)(2) - 1 - 2 \\
&= 2 + 6 - 1 - 2 \\
&= 8 - 1 - 2 \\
&= 7 - 2 \\
&= 5
\end{aligned}
$$

16. B: To factor the polynomial, find factors of the first and third term whose product can be added to get the middle term. Here, the factors 7 and -8 have a product of -56, and when added together yield -1. Another way to find the correct answer is to multiply the answer choices and select the choice that yields the original equation. In this case:

$$(x + 7)(x - 8) = (x)(x) + (x)(-8) + (7)(x) + (7)(-8)$$

$$= x^2 - 8x + 7x - 56$$

$$= x^2 - x - 56$$

- 145 -

17. D: The solution to the equation follows:

$$x^2 - 25 = 0$$

$$x^2 = 25$$

$$x = \sqrt{25}$$

$$x = +5 \text{ and } -5$$

18. C: To simplify the polynomial, group and combine all terms of the same order.

$$4x^3 + 5x - x^3 + 2x^2 + 17 - 3x^3 + 5x - 2x^2 + 3$$

$$(4x^3 - x^3 - 3x^3) + (2x^2 - 2x^2) + (5x + 5x) + (17 + 3)$$

$$0 + 0 + 10x + 20$$

$$10(x + 2)$$

19. B: A mathematical operation is commutative if altering the order does not alter the result of the operation. In other words, $a + b = b + a$, or $ab = ba$. Answer B fits this definition.

20. C: The distributive property says that terms inside a set of parentheses can be multiplied by a factor outside the parentheses. In other words,

$a(b + c) = ab + ac$. Answer C fits this definition.

21. B: By definition, a linear function is a first degree polynomial function of one variable, and the data shown in Table 2 can be written as such. The variable is the number of hours practiced, and the score is a function of that variable.

22. A: In each case, the number of points scored (p) equals 3(h) + 2 where h is the number of hours practiced. For example, $8 = (3)(2) + 2$ and $14 = (3)(4) + 2$. For answers C and D, the points scored are not written as functions of the hours practiced.

23. D: The range consists of all the values of the dependent variable. In this case, the dependent variable is the number of points scored.

24. C: The domain consists of all the values of the independent variable. In this case, the independent variable is the number of hours practiced.

25. B: The bar graph shown in Figure 2 is the only graph where the number of points scored corresponds to the number of hours practiced as presented in Table 2.

26. C: The slope of a line describes the change in the dependent variable divided by the change in the independent variable, i.e. the change in y over the change in x. To calculate the slope, consider any two points on the line. Let the first point be (1, 14), and let the second point be (2, 28).

$$\frac{y_2 - y_1}{x_2 - x_1} = \frac{28 - 14}{2 - 1} = \frac{14}{1} = 14$$

27. C: The slope of the line is the change in y divided by the change in x. Therefore, the units of the slope are the units of y over the units for x. The unit for y is the unit for distance or meters. The unit for x is the unit for time or seconds. Hence the units of the slope are meters over second or meters per second.

28. A: The slope describes the change in distance over the change in time. The change in distance over the change in time is a measure of the cheetah's speed in meters per second.

29. D: First write Equation A in slope-intercept form: $y = mx + b$ where b is the y-intercept and m is the slope:

$$10y - 5x = 40$$
$$10y = 5x + 40$$
$$y = 0.5x + 4$$

Based on the slope-intercept form of Equation A, the y-intercept b = 4, and the slope

$m = 0.5$.

30. A: Write Equation B in slope-intercept form, $y = mx + b$:

$$10y - 10x = 20$$
$$10y = 10x + 20$$
$$y = x + 2$$

Based on the slope-intercept form of Equation B, the slope is 1, which is twice the slope of Equation A.

31. C: Based on the slope-intercept form of Equation B, the y-intercept is 2, which is half the y-intercept of Equation A.

32. B: The slope of a line is the change in y divided by the change in x. Calculate the slope as follows:

$$m = \frac{y_2 - y_1}{x_2 - x_1}$$

$$m = \frac{75 - 30}{8 - 3}$$

$$m = \frac{45}{5}$$

$$m = 9$$

33. D: Write the equation in slope-intercept form: $y = mx + b$ where m is the slope of the line and b is the y-intercept. In this case, the slope m = 20 and the y-intercept b = 100. Hence $y = 20x + 1000$.

34. A: At the intersection point of line 1 and line 2, $y_1 = y_2 = y$ and

$x_1 = x_2 = x$. To find the x coordinate, let $y_1 = y_2$.

$$8x - 16 = -4x + 20$$
$$8x + 4x = 16 + 20$$
$$12x = 36$$
$$x = 3$$

Now find the y coordinate by substituting x = 3 into either the equation for line 1 or the equation for line 2:

$$y = -4x + 20$$

$$y = (-4)(3) + 20$$

$$y = -12 + 20$$

$$y = 8$$

Therefore, the point of intersection is (3, 8).

35. B: The intersection point of line P and line Q will be common to both lines. See the explanation for question 34. Point (-9, -56) is the only point that is common to both lines.

36. A: Since Vivian will plant a total of 40 vegetables, the number of tomatoes plus the number of cucumbers is 40 or $T + C = 40$. Each tomato costs $1; so multiply the number of tomatoes by 1. Each cucumber costs $3; so multiply the number of cucumbers by 3. Vivian has a total of $80 to spend on tomatoes and cucumbers. So $T + 3C = 80$.

37. B: Use a linear system of equations to find the number of tomatoes. See the explanation for question 36. In this case, the system of equations is $T + C = 40$ and

$T + 3C = 80$. Begin with $T + C = 40$ and solve for C:

$$T + C = 40$$
$$C = 40 - T$$

Now substitute the equation for C into the equation $T + 3C = 80$:

$$T + 3C = 80$$
$$T + 3(40 - T) = 80$$
$$T + 120 - 3T = 80$$
$$-2T = -40$$
$$T = 20$$

Therefore, Vivian will plant 20 tomato bushes in her garden.

38. B: Based on previous work, the number of tomatoes T = 20 and $T + C = 40$. Therefore, $C = 40 - 20 = 20$. Hence, Vivian will plant 20 cucumber bushes in her garden.

39. C: Despite the price difference, Vivian will purchase 20 tomatoes and 20 cucumbers. B and C are incorrect because no information is given about the space the vegetables require or Vivian's vegetable preference.

40. D: The new amount of space requires defining a new system of equations. Vivian will now plant a total of 50 vegetables. Hence:

$$T + C = 50$$
$$C = 50 - T$$

Therefore:

$$T + 3C = 80$$
$$T + 3(50 - T) = 80$$
$$T + 150 - 3T = 80$$
$$-2T = -70$$
$$T = 35$$

When she has more space, Vivian will plant 35 tomato bushes in her garden. Since

$T + C = 50$, Vivian will plant 15 cucumber bushes in her garden.

41. A: In order to determine the number of questions Matthew must answer correctly, consider the number of points he must earn. Matthew will receive 3 points for each question he answers correctly, and x represents the number of questions. Therefore, Matthew will receive a total of 3x points for all the questions he answers correctly. Matthew must earn more than 96 points. Therefore, to determine the number of questions he must answer correctly, solve the inequality $3x > 96$.

42. C: First solve for the number of questions Matthew must answer correctly. See the explanation for question 41. To determine the number of correct answers Matthew needs, solve the following inequality:

$$3x > 96$$
$$x > \frac{96}{3}$$
$$x > 32$$

Therefore, Matthew must correctly answer at more than 32 questions to qualify for varsity sports. Since the test has 40 questions, he must answer less than 8 questions incorrectly. Matthew could also answer 0 questions incorrectly. Hence, the best inequality to describe the number of questions Matthew can answer incorrectly is $0 \leq x < 8$.

43. C: The inequality that best represents the number of questions Matthew can answer incorrectly is $0 \leq x < 8$. Hence, the left endpoint of the graph is 0, and the right endpoint is 8. Because Matthew can answer less than 8 questions incorrectly, the endpoint at 8 is not included in the data set and is represented by an open circle.

44. B: According to the statement of the problem, Matthew must earn more than 96 points. Therefore, answers C and D are incorrect. Furthermore, answer A is incorrect because this answer says his score can equal 96 points but Matthew needs more than 96 points. Because the test has a total of 40 questions, and each question is worth 3 points, Matthew can earn a maximum of (3)(40) or 120 points. Hence the best inequality is $96 \leq p < 120$.

45. C: Answers A and B are incorrect because Matthew must earn more than 96 points, which means he must correctly answer more than 32 questions. Answer D is incorrect because the problem statement mentions nothing about Matthew's desire to work a part-time job.

46. D: The range is all the y values. Refer to a graph of y_1 shown below.

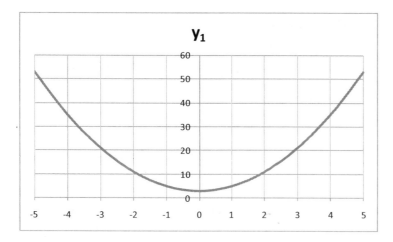

The minimum value for y is 3. Another way to solve this problem is to substitute the potential y values in the equation for y_1. For example,

$$y_1 = 2x^2 + 3$$
$$0 = 2x^2 + 3$$
$$-\frac{3}{2} = x^2$$
$$\sqrt{-\frac{3}{2}} = x$$

This statement has no real solution since it requires taking the square root of a negative number. Similar solutions are obtained if $y = 1$ or if $y = 2$.

47. B: The original function y_1 is concave up. See the graph of y_1 shown in the explanation for problem 46. Changing the coefficient of x^2 from +2 to -2 causes the function to be concave down. See the graph of y_2 shown below.

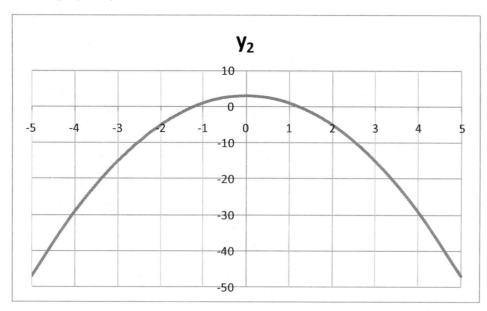

The y values for y_2 are different from those of y_1. Therefore, y_2 has a different range than y_1.

48. B: For function y_1, the y-intercept is +3. See the graph of y_1 shown in the explanation for problem 46. For function y_3, the y-intercept is -3. See the graph of y_3 shown below.

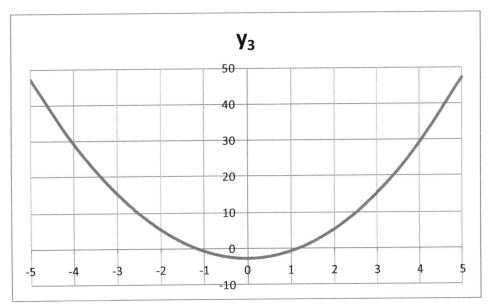

The graph of y_3 is similar to that of y_1 except the y-intercept of y_3 is 6 units below that of y_1. In other words, the difference between +3 and -3 is 6 units.

49. A: The graphs for y_1, y_2, and y_3 are displayed in the explanations for questions 46 – 48.

50. The correct answer is $x = -2$. The solution follows:

$$x^2 + 4x = -4$$
$$x^2 + 4x + 4 = 0$$
$$(x + 2)(x + 2) = 0$$
$$x + 2 = 0$$
$$x = -2$$

51. The correct answer is $x = -2$. The x-intercept is determined by setting the equation equal to zero and then solving for x. When $x^2 + 4x + 4 = 0$, then $x = -2$.

52. The correct answer is $x = -1$. The magnitude of x remains the same regardless of the power to which x is raised. Only 1 can be multiplied by itself several times and remain unchanged. The sign, however, alternates between positive and negative. Therefore, x must be -1. Note that multiplying a negative number by itself an even number of times yields a positive number. Multiplying a negative number by itself an odd number of times yields a negative number.

53. The correct answer is $x = -27$. The solution follows:

$$y = -\frac{1}{3}x$$

$$3y = -x$$

$$-3y = x$$

$$(-3)(9) = x$$

$$-27 = x$$

- 151 -

54. The correct answer is $x = 12$. The solution follows:

$$2^x = 4096$$

$$x \log 2 = \log 4096$$

$$x = \frac{\log 4096}{\log 2}$$

$$x = 12$$

How to Overcome Test Anxiety

Just the thought of taking a test is enough to make most people a little nervous. A test is an important event that can have a long-term impact on your future, so it's important to take it seriously and it's natural to feel anxious about performing well. But just because anxiety is normal, that doesn't mean that it's helpful in test taking, or that you should simply accept it as part of your life. Anxiety can have a variety of effects. These effects can be mild, like making you feel slightly nervous, or severe, like blocking your ability to focus or remember even a simple detail.

If you experience test anxiety—whether severe or mild—it's important to know how to beat it. To discover this, first you need to understand what causes test anxiety.

Causes of Test Anxiety

While we often think of anxiety as an uncontrollable emotional state, it can actually be caused by simple, practical things. One of the most common causes of test anxiety is that a person does not feel adequately prepared for their test. This feeling can be the result of many different issues such as poor study habits or lack of organization, but the most common culprit is time management. Starting to study too late, failing to organize your study time to cover all of the material, or being distracted while you study will mean that you're not well prepared for the test. This may lead to cramming the night before, which will cause you to be physically and mentally exhausted for the test. Poor time management also contributes to feelings of stress, fear, and hopelessness as you realize you are not well prepared but don't know what to do about it.

Other times, test anxiety is not related to your preparation for the test but comes from unresolved fear. This may be a past failure on a test, or poor performance on tests in general. It may come from comparing yourself to others who seem to be performing better or from the stress of living up to expectations. Anxiety may be driven by fears of the future—how failure on this test would affect your educational and career goals. These fears are often completely irrational, but they can still negatively impact your test performance.

> **Review Video:** 3 Reasons You Have Test Anxiety
> Visit mometrix.com/academy and enter code: 428468

Elements of Test Anxiety

As mentioned earlier, test anxiety is considered to be an emotional state, but it has physical and mental components as well. Sometimes you may not even realize that you are suffering from test anxiety until you notice the physical symptoms. These can include trembling hands, rapid heartbeat, sweating, nausea, and tense muscles. Extreme anxiety may lead to fainting or vomiting. Obviously, any of these symptoms can have a negative impact on testing. It is important to recognize them as soon as they begin to occur so that you can address the problem before it damages your performance.

> **Review Video:** <u>3 Ways to Tell You Have Test Anxiety</u>
> Visit mometrix.com/academy and enter code: 927847

The mental components of test anxiety include trouble focusing and inability to remember learned information. During a test, your mind is on high alert, which can help you recall information and stay focused for an extended period of time. However, anxiety interferes with your mind's natural processes, causing you to blank out, even on the questions you know well. The strain of testing during anxiety makes it difficult to stay focused, especially on a test that may take several hours. Extreme anxiety can take a huge mental toll, making it difficult not only to recall test information but even to understand the test questions or pull your thoughts together.

> **Review Video:** <u>How Test Anxiety Affects Memory</u>
> Visit mometrix.com/academy and enter code: 609003

Effects of Test Anxiety

Test anxiety is like a disease—if left untreated, it will get progressively worse. Anxiety leads to poor performance, and this reinforces the feelings of fear and failure, which in turn lead to poor performances on subsequent tests. It can grow from a mild nervousness to a crippling condition. If allowed to progress, test anxiety can have a big impact on your schooling, and consequently on your future.

Test anxiety can spread to other parts of your life. Anxiety on tests can become anxiety in any stressful situation, and blanking on a test can turn into panicking in a job situation. But fortunately, you don't have to let anxiety rule your testing and determine your grades. There are a number of relatively simple steps you can take to move past anxiety and function normally on a test and in the rest of life.

> **Review Video:** <u>How Test Anxiety Impacts Your Grades</u>
> Visit mometrix.com/academy and enter code: 939819

Physical Steps for Beating Test Anxiety

While test anxiety is a serious problem, the good news is that it can be overcome. It doesn't have to control your ability to think and remember information. While it may take time, you can begin taking steps today to beat anxiety.

Just as your first hint that you may be struggling with anxiety comes from the physical symptoms, the first step to treating it is also physical. Rest is crucial for having a clear, strong mind. If you are tired, it is much easier to give in to anxiety. But if you establish good sleep habits, your body and mind will be ready to perform optimally, without the strain of exhaustion. Additionally, sleeping well helps you to retain information better, so you're more likely to recall the answers when you see the test questions.

Getting good sleep means more than going to bed on time. It's important to allow your brain time to relax. Take study breaks from time to time so it doesn't get overworked, and don't study right before bed. Take time to rest your mind before trying to rest your body, or you may find it difficult to fall asleep.

> **Review Video: The Importance of Sleep for Your Brain**
> Visit mometrix.com/academy and enter code: 319338

Along with sleep, other aspects of physical health are important in preparing for a test. Good nutrition is vital for good brain function. Sugary foods and drinks may give a burst of energy but this burst is followed by a crash, both physically and emotionally. Instead, fuel your body with protein and vitamin-rich foods.

Also, drink plenty of water. Dehydration can lead to headaches and exhaustion, especially if your brain is already under stress from the rigors of the test. Particularly if your test is a long one, drink water during the breaks. And if possible, take an energy-boosting snack to eat between sections.

> **Review Video: How Diet Can Affect your Mood**
> Visit mometrix.com/academy and enter code: 624317

Along with sleep and diet, a third important part of physical health is exercise. Maintaining a steady workout schedule is helpful, but even taking 5-minute study breaks to walk can help get your blood pumping faster and clear your head. Exercise also releases endorphins, which contribute to a positive feeling and can help combat test anxiety.

When you nurture your physical health, you are also contributing to your mental health. If your body is healthy, your mind is much more likely to be healthy as well. So take time to rest, nourish your body with healthy food and water, and get moving as much as possible. Taking these physical steps will make you stronger and more able to take the mental steps necessary to overcome test anxiety.

> **Review Video: How to Stay Healthy and Prevent Test Anxiety**
> Visit mometrix.com/academy and enter code: 877894

Mental Steps for Beating Test Anxiety

Working on the mental side of test anxiety can be more challenging, but as with the physical side, there are clear steps you can take to overcome it. As mentioned earlier, test anxiety often stems from lack of preparation, so the obvious solution is to prepare for the test. Effective studying may be the most important weapon you have for beating test anxiety, but you can and should employ several other mental tools to combat fear.

First, boost your confidence by reminding yourself of past success—tests or projects that you aced. If you're putting as much effort into preparing for this test as you did for those, there's no reason you should expect to fail here. Work hard to prepare; then trust your preparation.

Second, surround yourself with encouraging people. It can be helpful to find a study group, but be sure that the people you're around will encourage a positive attitude. If you spend time with others who are anxious or cynical, this will only contribute to your own anxiety. Look for others who are motivated to study hard from a desire to succeed, not from a fear of failure.

Third, reward yourself. A test is physically and mentally tiring, even without anxiety, and it can be helpful to have something to look forward to. Plan an activity following the test, regardless of the outcome, such as going to a movie or getting ice cream.

When you are taking the test, if you find yourself beginning to feel anxious, remind yourself that you know the material. Visualize successfully completing the test. Then take a few deep, relaxing breaths and return to it. Work through the questions carefully but with confidence, knowing that you are capable of succeeding.

Developing a healthy mental approach to test taking will also aid in other areas of life. Test anxiety affects more than just the actual test—it can be damaging to your mental health and even contribute to depression. It's important to beat test anxiety before it becomes a problem for more than testing.

> **Review Video:** <u>**Test Anxiety and Depression**</u>
> Visit mometrix.com/academy and enter code: 904704

Study Strategy

Being prepared for the test is necessary to combat anxiety, but what does being prepared look like? You may study for hours on end and still not feel prepared. What you need is a strategy for test prep. The next few pages outline our recommended steps to help you plan out and conquer the challenge of preparation.

Step 1: Scope Out the Test

Learn everything you can about the format (multiple choice, essay, etc.) and what will be on the test. Gather any study materials, course outlines, or sample exams that may be available. Not only will this help you to prepare, but knowing what to expect can help to alleviate test anxiety.

Step 2: Map Out the Material

Look through the textbook or study guide and make note of how many chapters or sections it has. Then divide these over the time you have. For example, if a book has 15 chapters and you have five days to study, you need to cover three chapters each day. Even better, if you have the time, leave an extra day at the end for overall review after you have gone through the material in depth.

If time is limited, you may need to prioritize the material. Look through it and make note of which sections you think you already have a good grasp on, and which need review. While you are studying, skim quickly through the familiar sections and take more time on the challenging parts. Write out your plan so you don't get lost as you go. Having a written plan also helps you feel more in control of the study, so anxiety is less likely to arise from feeling overwhelmed at the amount to cover.

Step 3: Gather Your Tools

Decide what study method works best for you. Do you prefer to highlight in the book as you study and then go back over the highlighted portions? Or do you type out notes of the important information? Or is it helpful to make flashcards that you can carry with you? Assemble the pens, index cards, highlighters, post-it notes, and any other materials you may need so you won't be distracted by getting up to find things while you study.

If you're having a hard time retaining the information or organizing your notes, experiment with different methods. For example, try color-coding by subject with colored pens, highlighters, or post-it notes. If you learn better by hearing, try recording yourself reading your notes so you can listen while in the car, working out, or simply sitting at your desk. Ask a friend to quiz you from your flashcards, or try teaching someone the material to solidify it in your mind.

Step 4: Create Your Environment

It's important to avoid distractions while you study. This includes both the obvious distractions like visitors and the subtle distractions like an uncomfortable chair (or a too-comfortable couch that makes you want to fall asleep). Set up the best study environment possible: good lighting and a comfortable work area. If background music helps you focus, you may want to turn it on, but otherwise keep the room quiet. If you are using a computer to take notes, be sure you don't have any other windows open, especially applications like social media, games, or anything else that could distract you. Silence your phone and turn off notifications. Be sure to keep water close by so you stay hydrated while you study (but avoid unhealthy drinks and snacks).

Also, take into account the best time of day to study. Are you freshest first thing in the morning? Try to set aside some time then to work through the material. Is your mind clearer in the afternoon or evening? Schedule your study session then. Another method is to study at the same time of day that you will take the test, so that your brain gets used to working on the material at that time and will be ready to focus at test time.

Step 5: Study!

Once you have done all the study preparation, it's time to settle into the actual studying. Sit down, take a few moments to settle your mind so you can focus, and begin to follow your study plan. Don't give in to distractions or let yourself procrastinate. This is your time to prepare so you'll be ready to fearlessly approach the test. Make the most of the time and stay focused.

Of course, you don't want to burn out. If you study too long you may find that you're not retaining the information very well. Take regular study breaks. For example, taking five minutes out of every hour to walk briskly, breathing deeply and swinging your arms, can help your mind stay fresh.

As you get to the end of each chapter or section, it's a good idea to do a quick review. Remind yourself of what you learned and work on any difficult parts. When you feel that you've mastered the material, move on to the next part. At the end of your study session, briefly skim through your notes again.

But while review is helpful, cramming last minute is NOT. If at all possible, work ahead so that you won't need to fit all your study into the last day. Cramming overloads your brain with more information than it can process and retain, and your tired mind may struggle to recall even previously learned information when it is overwhelmed with last-minute study. Also, the urgent nature of cramming and the stress placed on your brain contribute to anxiety. You'll be more likely to go to the test feeling unprepared and having trouble thinking clearly.

So don't cram, and don't stay up late before the test, even just to review your notes at a leisurely pace. Your brain needs rest more than it needs to go over the information again. In fact, plan to finish your studies by noon or early afternoon the day before the test. Give your brain the rest of the day to relax or focus on other things, and get a good night's sleep. Then you will be fresh for the test and better able to recall what you've studied.

Step 6: Take a practice test

Many courses offer sample tests, either online or in the study materials. This is an excellent resource to check whether you have mastered the material, as well as to prepare for the test format and environment.

Check the test format ahead of time: the number of questions, the type (multiple choice, free response, etc.), and the time limit. Then create a plan for working through them. For example, if you have 30 minutes to take a 60-question test, your limit is 30 seconds per question. Spend less time on the questions you know well so that you can take more time on the difficult ones.

If you have time to take several practice tests, take the first one open book, with no time limit. Work through the questions at your own pace and make sure you fully understand them. Gradually work up to taking a test under test conditions: sit at a desk with all study materials put away and set a timer. Pace yourself to make sure you finish the test with time to spare and go back to check your answers if you have time.

After each test, check your answers. On the questions you missed, be sure you understand why you missed them. Did you misread the question (tests can use tricky wording)? Did you forget the information? Or was it something you hadn't learned? Go back and study any shaky areas that the practice tests reveal.

Taking these tests not only helps with your grade, but also aids in combating test anxiety. If you're already used to the test conditions, you're less likely to worry about it, and working through tests until you're scoring well gives you a confidence boost. Go through the practice tests until you feel comfortable, and then you can go into the test knowing that you're ready for it.

Test Tips

On test day, you should be confident, knowing that you've prepared well and are ready to answer the questions. But aside from preparation, there are several test day strategies you can employ to maximize your performance.

First, as stated before, get a good night's sleep the night before the test (and for several nights before that, if possible). Go into the test with a fresh, alert mind rather than staying up late to study.

Try not to change too much about your normal routine on the day of the test. It's important to eat a nutritious breakfast, but if you normally don't eat breakfast at all, consider eating just a protein bar. If you're a coffee drinker, go ahead and have your normal coffee. Just make sure you time it so that the caffeine doesn't wear off right in the middle of your test. Avoid sugary beverages, and drink enough water to stay hydrated but not so much that you need a restroom break 10 minutes into the test. If your test isn't first thing in the morning, consider going for a walk or doing a light workout before the test to get your blood flowing.

Allow yourself enough time to get ready, and leave for the test with plenty of time to spare so you won't have the anxiety of scrambling to arrive in time. Another reason to be early is to select a good seat. It's helpful to sit away from doors and windows, which can be distracting. Find a good seat, get out your supplies, and settle your mind before the test begins.

When the test begins, start by going over the instructions carefully, even if you already know what to expect. Make sure you avoid any careless mistakes by following the directions.

Then begin working through the questions, pacing yourself as you've practiced. If you're not sure on an answer, don't spend too much time on it, and don't let it shake your confidence. Either skip it and come back later, or eliminate as many wrong answers as possible and guess among the remaining ones. Don't dwell on these questions as you continue—put them out of your mind and focus on what lies ahead.

Be sure to read all of the answer choices, even if you're sure the first one is the right answer. Sometimes you'll find a better one if you keep reading. But don't second-guess yourself if you do immediately know the answer. Your gut instinct is usually right. Don't let test anxiety rob you of the information you know.

If you have time at the end of the test (and if the test format allows), go back and review your answers. Be cautious about changing any, since your first instinct tends to be correct, but make sure you didn't misread any of the questions or accidentally mark the wrong answer choice. Look over any you skipped and make an educated guess.

At the end, leave the test feeling confident. You've done your best, so don't waste time worrying about your performance or wishing you could change anything. Instead, celebrate the successful completion of this test. And finally, use this test to learn how to deal with anxiety even better next time.

> **Review Video:** <u>5 Tips to Beat Test Anxiety</u>
> Visit mometrix.com/academy and enter code: 570656

Important Qualification

Not all anxiety is created equal. If your test anxiety is causing major issues in your life beyond the classroom or testing center, or if you are experiencing troubling physical symptoms related to your anxiety, it may be a sign of a serious physiological or psychological condition. If this sounds like your situation, we strongly encourage you to seek professional help.

How to Overcome Your Fear of Math

The word *math* is enough to strike fear into most hearts. How many of us have memories of sitting through confusing lectures, wrestling over mind-numbing homework, or taking tests that still seem incomprehensible even after hours of study? Years after graduation, many still shudder at these memories.

The fact is, math is not just a classroom subject. It has real-world implications that you face every day, whether you realize it or not. This may be balancing your monthly budget, deciding how many supplies to buy for a project, or simply splitting a meal check with friends. The idea of daily confrontations with math can be so paralyzing that some develop a condition known as *math anxiety*.

But you do NOT need to be paralyzed by this anxiety! In fact, while you may have thought all your life that you're not good at math, or that your brain isn't wired to understand it, the truth is that you may have been conditioned to think this way. From your earliest school days, the way you were taught affected the way you viewed different subjects. And the way math has been taught has changed.

Several decades ago, there was a shift in American math classrooms. The focus changed from traditional problem-solving to a conceptual view of topics, de-emphasizing the importance of learning the basics and building on them. The solid foundation necessary for math progression and confidence was undermined. Math became more of a vague concept than a concrete idea. Today, it is common to think of math, not as a straightforward system, but as a mysterious, complicated method that can't be fully understood unless you're a genius.

This is why you may still have nightmares about being called on to answer a difficult problem in front of the class. Math anxiety is a very real, though unnecessary, fear.

Math anxiety may begin with a single class period. Let's say you missed a day in 6th grade math and never quite understood the concept that was taught while you were gone. Since math is cumulative, with each new concept building on past ones, this could very well affect the rest of your math career. Without that one day's knowledge, it will be difficult to understand any other concepts that link to it. Rather than realizing that you're just missing one key piece, you may begin to believe that you're simply not capable of understanding math.

This belief can change the way you approach other classes, career options, and everyday life experiences, if you become anxious at the thought that math might be required. A student who loves science may choose a different path of study upon realizing that multiple math classes will be required for a degree. An aspiring medical student may hesitate at the thought of going through the necessary math classes. For some this anxiety escalates into a more extreme state known as *math phobia*.

Math anxiety is challenging to address because it is rooted deeply and may come from a variety of causes: an embarrassing moment in class, a teacher who did not explain concepts well and contributed to a shaky foundation, or a failed test that contributed to the belief of math failure.

These causes add up over time, encouraged by society's popular view that math is hard and unpleasant. Eventually a person comes to firmly believe that he or she is simply bad at math. This belief makes it difficult to grasp new concepts or even remember old ones. Homework and test grades begin to slip, which only confirms the belief. The poor performance is not due to lack of ability but is caused by math anxiety.

Math anxiety is an emotional issue, not a lack of intelligence. But when it becomes deeply rooted, it can become more than just an emotional problem. Physical symptoms appear. Blood pressure may rise and heartbeat may quicken at the sight of a math problem – or even the thought of math! This fear leads to a mental block. When someone with math anxiety is asked to perform a calculation, even a basic problem can seem overwhelming and impossible. The emotional and physical response to the thought of math prevents the brain from working through it logically.

The more this happens, the more a person's confidence drops, and the more math anxiety is generated. This vicious cycle must be broken!

The first step in breaking the cycle is to go back to very beginning and make sure you really understand the basics of how math works and why it works. It is not enough to memorize rules for multiplication and division. If you don't know WHY these rules work, your foundation will be shaky and you will be at risk of developing a phobia. Understanding mathematical concepts not only promotes confidence and security, but allows you to build on this understanding for new concepts. Additionally, you can solve unfamiliar problems using familiar concepts and processes.

Why is it that students in other countries regularly outperform American students in math? The answer likely boils down to a couple of things: the foundation of mathematical conceptual understanding and societal perception. While students in the US are not expected to *like* or *get* math, in many other nations, students are expected not only to understand math but also to excel at it.

Changing the American view of math that leads to math anxiety is a monumental task. It requires changing the training of teachers nationwide, from kindergarten through high school, so that they learn to teach the *why* behind math and to combat the wrong math views that students may develop. It also involves changing the stigma associated with math, so that it is no longer viewed as unpleasant and incomprehensible. While these are necessary changes, they are challenging and will take time. But in the meantime, math anxiety is not irreversible—it can be faced and defeated, one person at a time.

False Beliefs

One reason math anxiety has taken such hold is that several false beliefs have been created and shared until they became widely accepted. Some of these unhelpful beliefs include the following:

There is only one way to solve a math problem. In the same way that you can choose from different driving routes and still arrive at the same house, you can solve a math problem using different methods and still find the correct answer. A person who understands the reasoning behind math calculations may be able to look at an unfamiliar concept and find the right answer, just by applying logic to the knowledge they already have. This approach may be different than what is taught in the classroom, but it is still valid. Unfortunately, even many teachers view math as a subject where the best course of action is to memorize the rule or process for each problem rather than as a place for students to exercise logic and creativity in finding a solution.

Many people don't have a mind for math. A person who has struggled due to poor teaching or math anxiety may falsely believe that he or she doesn't have the mental capacity to grasp mathematical concepts. Most of the time, this is false. Many people find that when they are relieved of their math anxiety, they have more than enough brainpower to understand math.

Men are naturally better at math than women. Even though research has shown this to be false, many young women still avoid math careers and classes because of their belief that their math abilities are inferior. Many girls have come to believe that math is a male skill and have given up trying to understand or enjoy it.

Counting aids are bad. Something like counting on your fingers or drawing out a problem to visualize it may be frowned on as childish or a crutch, but these devices can help you get a tangible understanding of a problem or a concept.

Sadly, many students buy into these ideologies at an early age. A young girl who enjoys math class may be conditioned to think that she doesn't actually have the brain for it because math is for boys, and may turn her energies to other pursuits, permanently closing the door on a wide range of opportunities. A child who finds the right answer but doesn't follow the teacher's method may believe that he is doing it wrong and isn't good at math. A student who never had a problem with math before may have a poor teacher and become confused, yet believe that the problem is because she doesn't have a mathematical mind.

Students who have bought into these erroneous beliefs quickly begin to add their own anxieties, adapting them to their own personal situations:

I'll never use this in real life. A huge number of people wrongly believe that math is irrelevant outside the classroom. By adopting this mindset, they are handicapping themselves for a life in a mathematical world, as well as limiting their career choices. When they are inevitably faced with real-world math, they are conditioning themselves to respond with anxiety.

I'm not quick enough. While timed tests and quizzes, or even simply comparing yourself with other students in the class, can lead to this belief, speed is not an indicator of skill level. A person can work very slowly yet understand at a deep level.

If I can understand it, it's too easy. People with a low view of their own abilities tend to think that if they are able to grasp a concept, it must be simple. They cannot accept the idea that they are capable of understanding math. This belief will make it harder to learn, no matter how intelligent they are.

I just can't learn this. An overwhelming number of people think this, from young children to adults, and much of the time it is simply not true. But this mindset can turn into a self-fulfilling prophecy that keeps you from exercising and growing your math ability.

The good news is, each of these myths can be debunked. For most people, they are based on emotion and psychology, NOT on actual ability! It will take time, effort, and the desire to change, but change is possible. Even if you have spent years thinking that you don't have the capability to understand math, it is not too late to uncover your true ability and find relief from the anxiety that surrounds math.

Math Strategies

It is important to have a plan of attack to combat math anxiety. There are many useful strategies for pinpointing the fears or myths and eradicating them:

Go back to the basics. For most people, math anxiety stems from a poor foundation. You may think that you have a complete understanding of addition and subtraction, or even decimals and percentages, but make absolutely sure. Learning math is different from learning other subjects. For example, when you learn history, you study various time periods and places and events. It may be important to memorize dates or find out about the lives of famous people. When you move from US history to world history, there will be some overlap, but a large amount of the information will be new. Mathematical concepts, on the other hand, are very closely linked and highly dependent on each other. It's like climbing a ladder – if a rung is missing from your understanding, it may be difficult or impossible for you to climb any higher, no matter how hard you try. So go back and make sure your math foundation is strong. This may mean taking a remedial math course, going to a tutor to work through the shaky concepts, or just going through your old homework to make sure you really understand it.

Speak the language. Math has a large vocabulary of terms and phrases unique to working problems. Sometimes these are completely new terms, and sometimes they are common words, but are used differently in a math setting. If you can't speak the language, it will be very difficult to get a thorough understanding of the concepts. It's common for students to think that they don't understand math when they simply don't understand the vocabulary. The good news is that this is fairly easy to fix. Brushing up on any terms you aren't quite sure of can help bring the rest of the concepts into focus.

Check your anxiety level. When you think about math, do you feel nervous or uncomfortable? Do you struggle with feelings of inadequacy, even on concepts that you know you've already learned? It's important to understand your specific math anxieties, and what triggers them. When you catch yourself falling back on a false belief, mentally replace it with the truth. Don't let yourself believe that you can't learn, or that struggling with a concept means you'll never understand it. Instead, remind yourself of how much you've already learned and dwell on that past success. Visualize grasping the new concept, linking it to your old knowledge, and moving on to the next challenge. Also, learn how to manage anxiety when it arises. There are many techniques for coping with the irrational fears that rise to the surface when you enter the math classroom. This may include controlled breathing, replacing negative thoughts with positive ones, or visualizing success. Anxiety interferes with your ability to concentrate and absorb information, which in turn contributes to greater anxiety. If you can learn how to regain control of your thinking, you will be better able to pay attention, make progress, and succeed!

Don't go it alone. Like any deeply ingrained belief, math anxiety is not easy to eradicate. And there is no need for you to wrestle through it on your own. It will take time, and many people find that speaking with a counselor or psychiatrist helps. They can help you develop strategies for responding to anxiety and overcoming old ideas. Additionally, it can be very helpful to take a short course or seek out a math tutor to help you find and fix the missing rungs on your ladder and make sure that you're ready to progress to the next level. You can also find a number of math aids online: courses that will teach you mental devices for figuring out problems, how to get the most out of your math classes, etc.

Check your math attitude. No matter how much you want to learn and overcome your anxiety, you'll have trouble if you still have a negative attitude toward math. If you think it's too hard, or just have general feelings of dread about math, it will be hard to learn and to break through the anxiety. Work on cultivating a positive math attitude. Remind yourself that math is not just a hurdle to be cleared, but a valuable asset. When you view math with a positive attitude, you'll be much more likely to understand and even enjoy it. This is something you must do for yourself. You may find it helpful to visit with a counselor. Your tutor, friends, and family may cheer you on in your endeavors. But your greatest asset is yourself. You are inside your own mind – tell yourself what you need to hear. Relive past victories. Remind yourself that you are capable of understanding math. Root out any false beliefs that linger and replace them with positive truths. Even if it doesn't feel true at first, it will begin to affect your thinking and pave the way for a positive, anxiety-free mindset.

Aside from these general strategies, there are a number of specific practical things you can do to begin your journey toward overcoming math anxiety. Something as simple as learning a new note-taking strategy can change the way you approach math and give you more confidence and understanding. New study techniques can also make a huge difference.

Math anxiety leads to bad habits. If it causes you to be afraid of answering a question in class, you may gravitate toward the back row. You may be embarrassed to ask for help. And you may procrastinate on assignments, which leads to rushing through them at the last moment when it's too late to get a better understanding. It's important to identify your negative behaviors and replace them with positive ones:

Prepare ahead of time. Read the lesson before you go to class. Being exposed to the topics that will be covered in class ahead of time, even if you don't understand them perfectly, is extremely helpful in increasing what you retain from the lecture. Do your homework and, if you're still shaky, go over some extra problems. The key to a solid understanding of math is practice.

Sit front and center. When you can easily see and hear, you'll understand more, and you'll avoid the distractions of other students if no one is in front of you. Plus, you're more likely to be sitting with students who are positive and engaged, rather than others with math anxiety. Let their positive math attitude rub off on you.

Ask questions in class and out. If you don't understand something, just ask. If you need a more in-depth explanation, the teacher may need to work with you outside of class, but often it's a simple concept you don't quite understand, and a single question may clear it up. If you wait, you may not be able to follow the rest of the day's lesson. For extra help, most professors have office hours outside of class when you can go over concepts one-on-one to clear up any uncertainties. Additionally, there may be a *math lab* or study session you can attend for homework help. Take advantage of this.

Review. Even if you feel that you've fully mastered a concept, review it periodically to reinforce it. Going over an old lesson has several benefits: solidifying your understanding, giving you a confidence boost, and even giving some new insights into material that you're currently learning! Don't let yourself get rusty. That can lead to problems with learning later concepts.

Teaching Tips

While the math student's mindset is the most crucial to overcoming math anxiety, it is also important for others to adjust their math attitudes. Teachers and parents have an enormous influence on how students relate to math. They can either contribute to math confidence or math anxiety.

As a parent or teacher, it is very important to convey a positive math attitude. Retelling horror stories of your own bad experience with math will contribute to a new generation of math anxiety. Even if you don't share your experiences, others will be able to sense your fears and may begin to believe them.

Even a careless comment can have a big impact, so watch for phrases like *He's not good at math* or *I never liked math*. You are a crucial role model, and your children or students will unconsciously adopt your mindset. Give them a positive example to follow. Rather than teaching them to fear the math world before they even know it, teach them about all its potential and excitement.

Work to present math as an integral, beautiful, and understandable part of life. Encourage creativity in solving problems. Watch for false beliefs and dispel them. Cross the lines between subjects: integrate history, English, and music with math. Show students how math is used every day, and how the entire world is based on mathematical principles, from the pull of gravity to the shape of seashells. Instead of letting students see math as a necessary evil, direct them to view it as an imaginative, beautiful art form – an art form that they are capable of mastering and using.

Don't give too narrow a view of math. It is more than just numbers. Yes, working problems and learning formulas is a large part of classroom math. But don't let the teaching stop there. Teach students about the everyday implications of math. Show them how nature works according to the laws of mathematics, and take them outside to make discoveries of their own. Expose them to math-related careers by inviting visiting speakers, asking students to do research and presentations, and learning students' interests and aptitudes on a personal level.

Demonstrate the importance of math. Many people see math as nothing more than a required stepping stone to their degree, a nuisance with no real usefulness. Teach students that algebra is used every day in managing their bank accounts, in following recipes, and in scheduling the day's events. Show them how learning to do geometric proofs helps them to develop logical thinking, an invaluable life skill. Let them see that math surrounds them and is integrally linked to their daily lives: that weather predictions are based on math, that math was used to design cars and other machines, etc. Most of all, give them the tools to use math to enrich their lives.

Make math as tangible as possible. Use visual aids and objects that can be touched. It is much easier to grasp a concept when you can hold it in your hands and manipulate it, rather than just listening to the lecture. Encourage math outside of the classroom. The real world is full of measuring, counting, and calculating, so let students participate in this. Keep your eyes open for numbers and patterns to discuss. Talk about how scores are calculated in sports games and how far apart plants are placed in a garden row for maximum growth. Build the mindset that math is a normal and interesting part of daily life.

Finally, find math resources that help to build a positive math attitude. There are a number of books that show math as fascinating and exciting while teaching important concepts, for example: *The Math Curse; A Wrinkle in Time; The Phantom Tollbooth;* and *Fractals, Googols and Other Mathematical Tales.* You can also find a number of online resources: math puzzles and games, videos that show math in nature, and communities of math enthusiasts. On a local level, students can compete in a variety of math competitions with other schools or join a math club.

The student who experiences math as exciting and interesting is unlikely to suffer from math anxiety. Going through life without this handicap is an immense advantage and opens many doors that others have closed through their fear.

Self-Check

Whether you suffer from math anxiety or not, chances are that you have been exposed to some of the false beliefs mentioned above. Now is the time to check yourself for any errors you may have accepted. Do you think you're not wired for math? Or that you don't need to understand it since you're not planning on a math career? Do you think math is just too difficult for the average person?

Find the errors you've taken to heart and replace them with positive thinking. Are you capable of learning math? Yes! Can you control your anxiety? Yes! These errors will resurface from time to time, so be watchful. Don't let others with math anxiety influence you or sway your confidence. If you're having trouble with a concept, find help. Don't let it discourage you!

Create a plan of attack for defeating math anxiety and sharpening your skills. Do some research and decide if it would help you to take a class, get a tutor, or find some online resources to fine-tune your knowledge. Make the effort to get good nutrition, hydration, and sleep so that you are operating at full capacity. Remind yourself daily that you are skilled and that anxiety does not control you. Your mind is capable of so much more than you know. Give it the tools it needs to grow and thrive.

Thank You

We at Mometrix would like to extend our heartfelt thanks to you, our friend and patron, for allowing us to play a part in your journey. It is a privilege to serve people from all walks of life who are unified in their commitment to building the best future they can for themselves.

The preparation you devote to these important testing milestones may be the most valuable educational opportunity you have for making a real difference in your life. We encourage you to put your heart into it—that feeling of succeeding, overcoming, and yes, conquering will be well worth the hours you've invested.

We want to hear your story, your struggles and your successes, and if you see any opportunities for us to improve our materials so we can help others even more effectively in the future, please share that with us as well. **The team at Mometrix would be absolutely thrilled to hear from you!** So please, send us an email (support@mometrix.com) and let's stay in touch.

Additional Bonus Material

Due to our efforts to try to keep this book to a manageable length, we've created a link that will give you access to all of your additional bonus material.

Please visit http://www.mometrix.com/bonus948/flalgebrai to access the information.